HOW TO GROW

First published in Great Britain in 2017 by Orion Spring,
an imprint of the Orion Publishing Group Ltd
Carmelite House
50 Victoria Embankment
London EC4Y 0DZ
An Hachette UK Company

10 9 8 7 6 5 4 3 2 1

A CIP catalogue record for this book is available from the British Library.

ISBN: 978-1-4091-6932-1

Photography: Ria Osborne, with the exception of pages 5 (top), 7, 28 (right), 53 (bottom left), 75, 77, 79 (top right, bottom left), 89, 106, 111, 115, 124, 132, 137, 142, 183 (excluding top left), 199, 215 (excluding top left), 223, 233, 237, 241: Hollie Newton, and 59, 60, 175, 177, 191: Shutterstock
Floral illustrations: Mariana Rodrigues
Instructional ilustrations: Emanuel Santos
Design and art direction: Abi Hartshorne
Food styling: Beatrice Ferrante and Bee Berrie
Props styling: Giuliana Casarotti
Printed and bound in Italy

FSC
www.fsc.org
MIX
Paper from
responsible sources
FSC® C023419

www.orionbooks.co.uk

A guide for gardeners who
can't garden yet

Hollie Newton

S

CONTENTS

INTRODUCTION

This is a book for gardeners who can't garden yet.

People with ideas. Enthusiasm. And the foolish optimism of someone who has absolutely no idea what they're doing. Gardeners like me, when I started.

Not to alarm you, but I'm not actually a Gardener. Not a professional Gardener with a capital 'G' at any rate. I haven't taken a single horticultural course; instead, I've spent the past seven years monkeying about in my own garden, merrily making every faux pas it's possible to make, before learning and moving onto the next. With a little help from the following pages, you'll know roughly a thousand times more than I did when I started, learning from my own jam-fool mistakes without having to make them yourself. This is a book designed to be as unintimidating as it's possible to be while brandishing a sharp garden fork and an over-excitable nature.

The fact is, I'm still learning – I always will be. And what could be better than that? Gardening shouldn't be the preserve of the expert. To shamelessly paraphrase Nigella Lawson, 'if you needed a professional qualification to [grow stuff], human beings would have fallen out of the evolutionary loop a long time ago.'

Your first ever strawberry. Your first tiny courgette. Your first weirdo malformed potato . . . This is the stuff of proper contented human achievement.

So, this is a book about gardening. But this is also a book about happiness.

Not that I knew that when I started. I was on a far simpler mission at the time: write the definitive antidote to all the fusty old-man-grumbling-at-a-hyacinth gardening books in the world. When I began growing stuff, it was a choice between 1: a heavy tome filled with austere-sounding Latin names, 2: Alan Titchmarsh, or 3: phone your granddad. No offence to Alan, but I have absolutely no intention of fitting a novelty water feature into my tiny back garden. (Though a sparkly disco ball hanging from a tree? That's another matter.)

Now I don't know if you've ever attempted to write a book before, but fook me, it's a big job. As I sat down to turn almost a decade's-worth of gardening potterings into some sort of coherent structure I turned, perhaps inevitably, to my photos. All 1.5GB of them. Photos taken in our garden. Photos of friends. Of each other. Of BBQs and birthdays. Vegetable triumphs and failures. Mum and Dad helping us to build the shed. Drinks in the last of the day's sun. Drinks well after the last of the day's sun. From our first tiny rented balcony – our downstairs neighbour shouting at his shoes, as I learnt to grow tumbling tomatoes and nearly successful raspberries – to our current little garden, these were memories of our happiest times. Small, quiet, personal happiness found, quite literally, in our own back yard.

This is perhaps the most unexpected thing that I've found as I've taught myself how to grow. Spend a few hours a week pootling about with plants and you won't simply have created something lovely to look at, won't only have created your own food from scratch; you will have created a small slice of contentment. From the very first morning that you spend up to your elbows in mud, a change occurs. A proper connection with the natural world, re-discovered, right in the heart of your little human soul. This is a happiness we can all enjoy. A genuine escape from an absurdly fast and stressful life.

And life truly is absurdly fast and stressful at the moment. Ludicrous working hours, non-existent job security, standard of life steadily dropping as the cost of living resolutely rises. Add an average of eight hours and 41 minutes per day lived in front of a digital screen and it's little wonder that anxiety and depression are at an all-time high.

In the UK, 70 per cent of working adults in their late 20s and early 30s say their emotional health has deteriorated since 2005; an enormous 60 per cent of all working adults, when you take every age group into account. That's roughly 19 million of us in Britain alone putting a brave face on things every day.

This steady decline in happiness seems to me to go hand-in-hand with our continued removal from the natural world. Perhaps unsurprisingly, hours spent in front of a computer screen in an air-conditioned office are not conducive to happiness. As Hugo Bugg, the 2014 Chelsea Flower Show's youngest winner in over two decades, so eloquently put it, 'people look out of the window and see the sun shining, and they just want to put away their screens and be with nature.'

As a Dorset lass who's worked in London for over a decade, the natural world has seemed a long way away at times. I've spent much of my adult life attempting to wrestle near-obliterating depression to the floor and, unexpectedly, covering myself in compost while trying to coax a Brussels sprout from a misbehaving brassica is one of the few things that's genuinely helped. Saved me, even.

Today, I arrived home late, half-crazed from commuter rage, genuinely concerned that I may be experiencing a low-level heart attack having discovered twenty-three new emails on my phone. I decided to ignore them, dropped my laptop and bags on the sofa, and stepped into the garden.

The last of the day's light hung low over the back of the house – flagstones still warm under my toes, the scent of tumbling honeysuckle mixing with an entire street's worth of summer evening BBQs – as I checked on the vegetables. There were courgettes ready to be harvested. Mangetout to tie back. And a caterpillar invasion to be dealt with. At some point, my husband, Tim pottered out with a bowl, reaching past me to pick tomatoes from the vine for dinner, as though it was the most natural thing in the world.

After a while I noticed two things: One. It had become so dark I couldn't see the mangetout in front of me. Two. I felt better. Calm. Relaxed. Covered in aphids . . . and happy.

It won't say as much in the following pages. You'll find helpful things instead, like how to plant beetroot, how to support cherry tomatoes, or how to grow yourself a constant supply of sweet peas. However, the effect is profound. There's more joy to be found in your first hilariously wonky carrot than a lifetime of Moschino jackets. A big claim, considering how much I love conspicuous 80s regalia.

The best thing of all? I don't live in a countryside idyll, rich in space and time. I live in London, in a garden flat (estate-agent speak for basement). Working 80 hours a week running a brilliant yet frantic creative agency. Our garden is small. Long and weirdly narrow. But it's our long and weirdly narrow garden, damn it. And we transformed it, all by ourselves, from post-apocalyptic wasteland, to a joyful, colourful, plant-filled sanctuary all our own.

Whatever space, time, or vague hint of ability you have, this book is written for you. From a small sunny windowsill, to the dark awkward corner you try not to look at from your window. This is the first step in a life-long love affair.

One last thing before we crack on. I'd like to reiterate perhaps the most important rule of gardening, in my opinion: there is absolutely nothing wrong with completely fudging up. The time I accidentally used neat tomato feed and fried the baby tomatoes. The time I got drunk, fell over, and broke the beetroot. The time the horseradish overpowered me and tried to take control of all that I held dear. Take this book as a jumping-off point; start with a few things that tickle your fancy, then go and commit some ingenious new fudge-ups all your own. Wear them with pride. Laugh. Then try again.

In fact, I'd love to hear about them. Share your failures on Instagram #HowToGrowBook @HollieNuisance and we can all commiserate together. Share your triumphs, too. I'm all for a distraction from work.

HOW TO USE THIS BOOK

Evidently, this is a book, so reading the words is an excellent idea. However, if, like me, you're a fickle look-at-the-pictures page flicker, fear not – I've made the important information as easy-to-digest as is humanly possible. From planning your garden and deciding what to grow, to keeping your plants alive, trouble-shooting and deciding what to make with your home-grown produce once you've picked it, you'll find everything you need to know to get growing. I've even broken it all down into handy chapters and sub-sections for you – perfect for dipping into and checking back on in the sunny months to come.

Try to behave yourself and resist skipping the first 'Before We Begin' chapter. This lays out everything you need to think about before you get over-excited in the garden centre and spend all your pocket money on unnecessary tools or easy-to-kill plants. You'll learn how to plan and design your garden, what you'll need to do to keep all your new plants alive and how to make your garden inviting to wildlife – even in the heart of the city.

The following herb, vegetable, salad, fruit and flower chapters will act both as inspiration for what to plant and as a detailed guide as to how to look after them – from planting all the way through to harvesting. I've arranged them within each chapter in order of when to plant them out, and it goes without saying that every plant is on the easy end of the growing scale. I don't want to see anyone crying into their veg patch at such an early stage of their growing careers.

You'll also find a handy key next to each plant . . .

ANNUAL, PERENNIAL, BIENNIAL — Whether the plant is annual, perennial or biennial, aka 'how long your plant will live'. An annual will grow and produce fruit or flowers in one season before falling over and dying; a biennial will grow in the first year then flower or fruit in the second year, then die; a perennial will grow and produce fruit and flowers every year, year after year after year. Like Morgan Freeman.

Whether you'll be planting from seeds, bulbs, seedlings or even, on occasion, young trees.

When to plant your seeds, bulbs, seedlings or plants.

How much sunshine your plant will need. Full sun means direct sunshine for 6–10 hours a day, partial shade means 3–6 hours direct sunshine per day, shade means pretty much never receiving a single shaft of unobscured sunlight.

How much space your plant will take up once fully grown.

When to pick your veg, fruit, salad, herbs and flowers.

WINDOWSILLS, BALCONIES, FRONT STEPS AND TINY SPACES

You'll find a ⬚ symbol in every section of this book. If you only have a tiny space, don't for a minute think you can't grow some damn fine vegetables. Even if you only get two hours of sun each day, there'll be something in here for you. If you only have a narrow windowsill, let me introduce you to trailing tomatoes, edible flowers and good old-fashioned herbs.

In short, don't panic; you can grow all sorts. Truth be told, with a little inspiration, a few pots will look far better than many of the big, soulless, professionally landscaped beds in the land. Here's to container gardening.

POTENTIAL DISASTERS

Not to alarm you, but there are all sorts of things that can go wrong with your plants – almost infinite ways in which Nature can come at you, and even more infinite (a million mathematicians just sighed) ways in which you can mess things up yourself. But don't worry; in each section, I'll be flagging the most prevalent problems/easily avoidable mistakes for each plant listed. These are usually things that I've got wrong myself; luckily I'm sharing my many mistakes so that you don't have to make them yourself. However, there are some general problems, too, that are common to all plants and so are worth mentioning here, such as keeping your beds weed-free and protecting your crops against marauding squirrels, mice and the Damn Pigeon.

There are also the myriad pests and diseases that could suddenly harass your precious garden (see page 28 for some tips to keep them at bay). My advice? Don't worry about it too much. If caught early, most things are fixable. And remember . . . if all is lost, have a strong drink, chalk it down to life's rich tapestry of learning through disaster and try again next year.

GARDENING WITHOUT A GARDEN

One last thing . . . What if you don't have any outside space at all?

I say, schnaffle some out. The shared gardens of an apartment block will have more than enough room for a vegetable patch. Go and pitch your heart out to the residents' association (I still, to this day, remember the never-ending notices from 'Residents' Chair, Peter Croissant' at an old Soho flat. That really was his name). Similarly, unused patches of land in the local area have huge potential. From the little squares of soil around the trees in pavements (people plant everything from pansies to beetroot in these near me. I've seen it with my own eyes), to bigger strips of neglected land in your local community. Helpfully, local transport and conservation trusts are increasingly supporting community groups wanting to turn these over to vegetables. In the UK, British Waterways, Network Rail and the National Trust are prime examples. Go seek them out.

BEFORE WE BEGIN

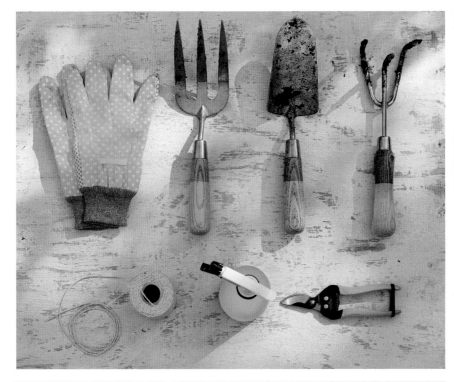

THE ESSENTIALS

Gardening can get expensive if you let your inner Michael Jackson take hold. There are so many shiny things to tempt you as soon as you set foot in a garden centre; so many 'must-have' tools, sprays, widgets and accessories. Ignore them all. The truth is, you need very little to get started, just these basics.

TOOLS AND KIT

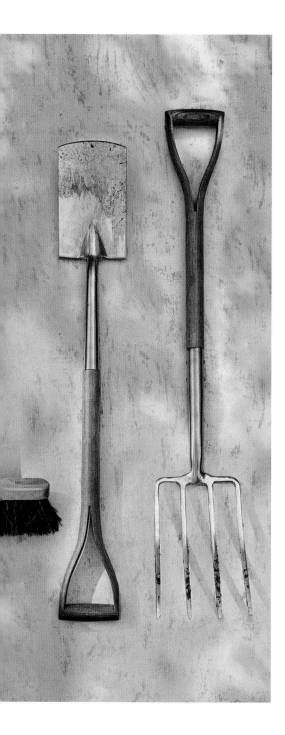

Thick gardening gloves – to protect your hands from scratches and accidentally caressing slugs.

A small garden trowel and fork – essential for every gardener.

A hand rake – makes weeding super quick and easy.

Garden twine – to tie up everything from beans to sweet peas.

A handheld waterspray bottle – for spraying everything from bug spray to tomato feed.

Sharp secateurs – for snipping, harvesting and pruning.

Bamboo canes – to construct supports for plants to grow up.

A garden broom – to sweep away leaves, etc. and keep surfaces tidy.

A big garden spade and fork – if you're lucky enough to have a garden with flowerbeds.

COMPOST AND FEED

Multipurpose peat-free compost – for using in beds.

Tomato feed – for pretty much all veg, not just for tomatoes.

Bonemeal – as a feed, in particular for roses and rhubarb.

Fertiliser pellets – to feed plants gradually over time.

Peat-free potting compost – for planting in pots.

WHAT TO PLANT WHEN

Here's every plant in the book, arranged into handy tables showing you when to plant and when to harvest.

The simple rule when choosing what you want to grow is, what do you fancy eating? What do you fancy looking at as you relax in the sunshine? What do you want to amaze your friends and family with when you rock up at Sunday lunch, arms laden with home-grown produce? Take the pick'n'mix approach, that's what I say.

However, there's something very important you should know before you flick through the following pages: I don't grow all of this every year. If only. Alas, I simply don't have the space. If I'd tried everything in the first year I would have been totally overwhelmed, had a breakdown somewhere between the carrots and the mangetout, and may never have written this book. Inadvertently saved by my miniscule garden once again. It's far better to plant a little too little than way too much.

HOW TO PLANT YOUR PLANT

Water your seedling with the fine spray of a watering can while he's still in his multi-celled tray or plastic pot. Then 'pop' him out by pushing your thumbs up underneath. If that doesn't work, a quick sharp tap with a trowel while holding the pot upside down should do the trick. Loosen your seedling's roots by teasing them out of their soil ball, then dig a hole in the soil, slightly larger than the pot he came in, and tuck your plant in, roots down. Fill the hole back in, firming the soil to ensure he doesn't wobble. Then it's one last water for luck.

KEY

Plant | Harvest/Pick | Chit

HERBS

	Page No.	JAN	FEB	MAR	APR	MAY	JUN	JUL	AUG	SEP	OCT	NOV	DEC
Chives	60			Plant	Plant	Plant	Plant	Harvest/Pick	Harvest/Pick	Harvest/Pick			
Lemon thyme	61	Harvest/Pick	Harvest/Pick	Harvest/Pick	Plant / Harvest/Pick	Plant / Harvest/Pick	Harvest/Pick	Harvest/Pick	Harvest/Pick	Harvest/Pick	Harvest/Pick	Harvest/Pick	Harvest/Pick
Bay tree	61	Harvest/Pick	Harvest/Pick	Harvest/Pick	Plant / Harvest/Pick	Plant / Harvest/Pick	Plant / Harvest/Pick	Plant / Harvest/Pick	Plant / Harvest/Pick	Plant / Harvest/Pick	Harvest/Pick	Harvest/Pick	Harvest/Pick
Mint	62	Harvest/Pick	Harvest/Pick	Harvest/Pick	Plant / Harvest/Pick	Plant / Harvest/Pick	Plant / Harvest/Pick	Plant / Harvest/Pick	Plant / Harvest/Pick	Plant / Harvest/Pick	Harvest/Pick	Harvest/Pick	Harvest/Pick
Basil	62					Plant / Harvest/Pick	Plant / Harvest/Pick	Plant / Harvest/Pick	Harvest/Pick	Harvest/Pick			
Rosemary	65	Harvest/Pick	Harvest/Pick	Harvest/Pick	Harvest/Pick	Plant / Harvest/Pick	Plant / Harvest/Pick	Plant / Harvest/Pick	Plant / Harvest/Pick	Plant / Harvest/Pick	Harvest/Pick	Harvest/Pick	Harvest/Pick
Sage	65	Harvest/Pick	Harvest/Pick	Harvest/Pick	Harvest/Pick	Plant / Harvest/Pick	Plant / Harvest/Pick	Plant / Harvest/Pick	Plant / Harvest/Pick	Plant / Harvest/Pick	Harvest/Pick	Harvest/Pick	Harvest/Pick

VEGETABLES

	Page No.	JAN	FEB	MAR	APR	MAY	JUN	JUL	AUG	SEP	OCT	NOV	DEC
Carrots	70			Plant	Plant	Plant / Harvest/Pick	Plant / Harvest/Pick	Harvest/Pick	Harvest/Pick	Harvest/Pick	Harvest/Pick	Harvest/Pick	
Horseradish	78	Harvest/Pick	Harvest/Pick	Plant	Plant	Plant						Harvest/Pick	Harvest/Pick
Potatoes	84	Chit	Chit	Plant	Plant		Harvest/Pick	Harvest/Pick	Harvest/Pick	Harvest/Pick	Harvest/Pick		
Beans: broad & runner	92				Plant	Plant	Plant / Harvest/Pick	Plant / Harvest/Pick	Harvest/Pick	Harvest/Pick			Harvest/Pick
Courgettes	102				Plant	Plant	Plant	Plant / Harvest/Pick	Harvest/Pick	Harvest/Pick	Harvest/Pick		
Peas: mangetout & sugarsnap	110				Plant	Plant	Harvest/Pick	Harvest/Pick	Harvest/Pick	Harvest/Pick			
Tomatoes	116				Plant	Plant	Plant	Harvest/Pick	Harvest/Pick	Harvest/Pick			
Beetroot	126					Plant	Plant	Plant / Harvest/Pick	Harvest/Pick	Harvest/Pick	Harvest/Pick	Harvest/Pick	

OVERWINTERING VEG

	Page No.	JAN	FEB	MAR	APR	MAY	JUN	JUL	AUG	SEP	OCT	NOV	DEC
Leeks	138					Harvest/Pick	Harvest/Pick			Plant	Plant		
Onions, shallots & garlic	144						Harvest/Pick	Harvest/Pick	Harvest/Pick	Plant	Plant	Plant	

SALAD

	Page No.	JAN	FEB	MAR	APR	MAY	JUN	JUL	AUG	SEP	OCT	NOV	DEC
Little gem Lettuce (aka cos)	156			■	■	■	■	■	■	■			
Rainbow chard	160			■	■	■	■	■	■				
Wild rocket	164			■	■		■	■	■	■	■	■	
Radishes	168				■	■	■	■	■				

FRUIT

	Page No.	JAN	FEB	MAR	APR	MAY	JUN	JUL	AUG	SEP	OCT	NOV	DEC
Strawberries	176					■	■	■	■				
Rhubarb	182					■	■				■	■	
Raspberries	190	■	■	■				■				■	■
Apple Tree	198	■	■	■				■	■	■		■	■

FLOWERS

	Page No.	JAN	FEB	MAR	APR	MAY	JUN	JUL	AUG	SEP	OCT	NOV	DEC
Edible flowers	210			■	■	■	■						
Nasturtiums	214			■	■	■	■	■					
Sweet peas	224				■	■	■	■	■				
Roses	220		■	■		■	■	■		■	■		
Hydrangeas	228						■	■	■	■	■		
Wild flowers	231									■	■		
Spring bulbs	232			■	■						■	■	■

SEEDLINGS

Ninety per cent of everything we'll be growing in this book will be started from pre-grown seedlings rather than seed. Also referred to as young plants, these are the little plants you find in multi-celled boxes and small plastic pots lined up in rows and rows at the garden centre, ready for you to take home and plant.

Now this is something that's left me wracked with worry over the years. If I use pre-grown seedlings, am I not a proper gardener? If I haven't grown every single thing from seed, am I a terrible horticultural cheat? The beetroot I've tended for five months; watered, fed, pruned and defended from slugs, dug up, washed and finally served for dinner, are they less of an achievement because they originally came from the grow-your-own section of a national DIY chain?

Of course they're ruddy not.

When you're starting out, you have neither the space, nor the money, for a greenhouse. (Oh, how I dream of the reliable and controllable growing conditions of a greenhouse. Or patio glasshouse. Or consistently sunny enormous bright windowsill.) But more than that, I truly believe that you've got enough to learn, experiment with and generally muck up without adding the pressure of sowing seeds into the mix. Give yourself a break.

There's a world of seedling options right on your doorstep (which rather indicates that we're not the only ones taking this shortcut), so we won't be stuck with boring varieties. Ladies and gentlemen, we're using seedlings.

N.B. On a few occasions, such as when growing wild rocket and meadow flowers, you'll see that I recommend seeds. Nobody panic – I'll only do this if seeds are the easiest, most prolific and economical way to go.

THINGS I WOULDN'T BLOODY

BOTHER WITH

GOOD LORD I've had some unmitigated disasters in my time. Yes, there's hilarity to be had in total failure (and an excuse for a vodka martini), but there are certain things I wish someone had told me when I first started out gardening.

Cauliflower, for instance. In the scheme of happy-go-lucky, easy-to-grow vegetables, cauliflower is on the Joan Collins end of demanding. Everything in the world wants to eat, infect or undermine it. It hates having too much sun. Or warmth. Or, conversely, heavy frost. It needs an outrageous amount of room to grow properly. And we're never speaking again. One site even said, 'best left to commercial growers'. THEN WHY IS IT IN THE GROW-YOUR-OWN SECTION? Cauliflower rage descends.

Similarly, Brussels sprouts are complete wankers. I had romantical ideas of growing them for Christmas dinner. How I laugh now. To say that caterpillars like them is to say that crack cocaine is a tad moreish. They were shredded, only to make a miraculous recovery, start to grow little Brussels sprouts balls . . . and then promptly unfurl their leaves in protest. *sigh*

Artichokes, aubergine, sweetcorn and celery are going to give you an equally hard time in your early gardening years. I say, start with the easy chaps. Happily, the plants featured in this book are just that.

LONG LIVE THE LOCAL
GARDEN CENTRE

Get to know your local independent garden centre. No longer the preserve of blue-rinsed retirees, the modern garden centre is a thing of calm escapist joy. W6, just under the railway arches by Ravenscourt Park, in London, is my local haunt – a dangerously close 10-minute walk from our flat.

In my experience, you can ask garden centre staff the most foolish questions in the world and they still won't laugh in your face. Not only will they give you advice and emotional support in times of garden woe, they'll also order in most things for you. Fancy a posh golden beetroot variety? They're on it. Need a carrot suitable for a shallow window box? No problem.

#THEINTERNETS

I don't know if you've heard of it, but The Internet is a wonderful place. It even sells real-life plants. There are all sorts of options, from small dedicated fruit and veg nurseries to the big 'uns – all of which have a huge range and can send everything from mangetout seedlings to a hazel tree through the post. The only thing I'd advise is that you place your order a good few weeks before you need your plants, as some of these small nurseries take things in their own sweet time. Oh . . . and make sure you'll be at home when they arrive. It won't surprise you to hear that a tray of sweet peas left in a hot cardboard box for three days will die a horrible death.

If, like many of my city dwelling friends, you don't own a car, or you live far away from a big garden centre, online ordering is in fact an absolute necessity. Take it from me, lugging three massive bags of compost home on a 40-minute bus journey involving three changes should be avoided at all costs.

THE BIG'UNS

And then, of course, there are the large DIY chain stores. Nothing wrong with these guys. Their grow-your-own ranges are getting bigger and bigger every year. When I started, I bought seedlings from UK institution Homebase. In fact, I still get my little yellow 'Taxi' courgette there every spring.

KEEPING YOUR PLANTS ALIVE, AKA WATERING

You'll find a section under each plant called 'Keeping them alive' (which is pretty important. No one wants a death in the family). Though each vegetable, fruit, etc. will have its own particular quirks, one thing is true of all plants . . . the need for water. It is, in fact, all about the soil. Not too dry, not too wet. Generally, the best way to tell is to stick your finger into the soil, just near the main stem of your plant. If it's moist, but not soggy, to the touch, it's right. Water your plants early in the morning, or from late afternoon onwards when the air is coolest, so that you don't lose water to evaporation. If it's been raining regularly, you probably won't need to water. If we're having a hot sunny spell, water twice a day. Simples.

N.B. If you notice me using terms such as 'a good water' or 'water well' when it comes to planting your seedlings, I mean giving them a proper drink to settle them in (the soil they come with is often very dry). About 30 seconds or so with a hose on sprinkle setting or watering can for each plant will do it.

NICE HOSE *FNAR*

If you're lucky enough to have an outside tap, treat yourself to a hose on one of those windy-round stands. It's so easy to step outside, turn it on and splash a bit of water on everything before work, then run out at the end of the day and do it again. I've taken conference calls in one hand while watering the garden with the other. We got a plumber to install an outdoor tap when we were doing up the flat. Like a real grown-up. I tend to use a wide sprinkler setting when watering, which covers a big area and doesn't blast little plants with too powerful and narrow a jet of water.

If you don't have an outside tap, DON'T PANIC. You can run an extra-long hose from an inside tap, out of a back door or window, or take a more old-fashioned approach . . . an enormous great watering can. This comes with the added benefit that you can tone your arm muscles at the same time as watering. I always go for a bright, colourful neon design (because I'm a ponce), but something with a wide head and big capacity will do. It's actually a good idea to have one on standby anyway, in case of hosepipe bans. Jennifer Aniston arm muscles all round.

Handy hint: One of the greatest pieces of advice my dad has ever given me is this: when you have plumber/electrician/'chap' in, think of every single job you could possibly want doing in the house – your main cost is calling them out in the first place. Paul the Plumber sorted out our outside tap while fixing the loo. Thanks, Paul.

PEST CONTROL

You know what, there's no real stopping the army of hungry little nuisances that you'll discover in your garden. And I'm not sure I'd feel comfortable with a full-scale chemical genocide – it's their garden too. In fact, many insects are remarkably beneficial. Aphid-munching ladybirds, pollinating honey bees, even wasps and certain beetles. However, sometimes action needs to be taken against the little rogues who are going to do your plants harm. The oldest, most organic tactic of all pest control is the simplest: companion planting . . .

1

COMPANION PLANTING

Companion planting, aka the selfless sacrifice of one plant for another. Some plants can be planted purely to lure dickhead pests away from your favourite crop. French marigold and mint (see page 62) are brilliant at deterring all sorts of harmful insects due to their pungent smell. Nasturtium (see page 214), on the other hand, does the exact opposite, attracting caterpillars away from your precious crop and sacrificing itself. What a hero. Pop a few of these in amongst your vegetable patch and they'll act like Kevin Costner in *The Bodyguard*.

Handy hint: To plant French marigolds, find a sunny spot in your veg patch and plant them 60cm apart. Water at the base of the plant rather than from overhead to get maximum water uptake, and deadhead regularly to ensure lots of new blooms.

2

SLUG PELLETS

Alas, I can't live without these. Having tried everything else, these bright blue specks are, in my experience, the only answer to the ever-advancing tide of hungry slugs towards my precious vegetables. However, there are options. Look out for those labelled as child and pet safe. You can even find organic options. Sprinkle generously around all newly planted seedlings and any particularly munchable plants such as rhubarb and beetroot and, well, everything really.

3

TIMMY'S HOMEMADE FLY-DESTROYING SPRAY OF AWESOMENESS

Greenfly, whitefly, tiny munching caterpillars – all dispatched with a single spray of Timmy's invention. I once drenched every inch of our rose in this when it was under heavy bombardment from roughly one million caterpillars. Miraculously, the rose survived. I didn't see another caterpillar all summer.

Why does Timmy's mix work so well? It's the combination of ingredients. The strong smell of the garlic and tobacco repels aphids and co.; coffee is poisonous to slugs and snails; chillies scorch the skin of soft-skinned/shelled pests and soap makes the mixture stick to the leaves of the plant. All without harming the crop you're protecting. Clever.

Here's what you'll need:

500ml tap water

3 garlic cloves, peeled and finely sliced

1 tsp coffee granules (not decaf)

3 dried chillies, crumbled

A dash of Tabasco

½ tsp washing-up liquid

Water/plant spray bottle

Mix together in a truly *George's Marvellous Medicine* manner and transfer to a spray bottle, laughing evilly as you go. Then spritz the affected area whenever you see a problem.

Handy hint: Never spray plants in hot, sunny weather or you may end up scorching the leaves. The cooler hours of morning and evening are best.

31

PLAN
NING
& DES
IGN

PLANNING AND DESIGN

Nobody panic. This isn't going to get hugely technical. I shan't be wielding a set square in one hand and a sharply pointed pair of compasses in the other. At most, we get to sit and doodle in the sunshine, dreaming up possibilities, while eating a cookie.

Alongside helpful advice on the basics of your space, such as light and shade, soil type and how to grow upwards when you've run out of room, I've also included some tempting (and easy) design ideas to help spark your inner Jean Paul Gaultier. Don't for a minute think that you have to stick to these. Go mad. Embark on your own gloriously harebrained schemes. The worst that can happen is that you have to paint over something or start again.

OVERPLANTING COMPULSION

DISORDER

Now listen up, and listen up good. I'm going to say this, and you're going to ignore it. Bloody hell, I'm going to say this and I'M going to ignore it. Don't get over excited and plant too much.

Seedlings go in small and come out big. VERY big. I've had tomatoes battling beans bullying beetroot harassing carrots knocking over potatoes committing genocide on the romaine lettuce. To help you avoid this fate, I've included a rough idea of how much space each plant will take up once it's fully grown. Also, bear in mind that the more you grow (particularly veg and fruit), the more time you'll need to spend tending them.

Flick through this book, pick your favourites, and write a list. DO NOT DEVIATE FROM THE LIST. She says, skipping off to Homebase, falling for the 8 for 2 offer. 'Ooh look! Purple sprouting broccoli . . .'

LIGHT AND SHADE

Before planting anything, it's important to know where your best and worst areas are in the garden in terms of positioning plants. Over a few days, keep an eye on where the sun rises, falls and casts its light throughout the day. Once you've worked this out, plant those that depend on full sunlight in the parts that get the most sun, and those that can cope with the dodgy shady end . . . well, in the dodgy shady end.

If you are a shade-plagued gardening fan, dry those tears, for all is not lost. It turns out, awkward shady spots can be transformed with a little clever thinking. Ferns, succulents and flowers (see living wall options – page 40) can be planted in big, brightly coloured planters, which will lighten up any shady corner. Woodland flowers like foxgloves (see page 240) and edible wild garlic love a dappled partly-in-shadow spot. Woodland-mix seeds can be sprinkled in the tiniest of dirt patches and become a tiny oasis of colour in only a few months, thanks to them evolving under the densely dappled light of trees.

Good old nature. Sorting us out again.

OVERWINTERING

What the fudge is overwintering? Clever. That's what. If only I'd cottoned onto it sooner.

You see, the thing about a garden in winter is . . . it's a bit rubbish. Cold, rainy, frosty. No more BBQs. No more pub shed (read on, grasshopper). Not much in the way of flowers. Truly, a state of not-much-going-on reigns.

And the veg patch? Well, suddenly, after clearing the last of the tomato plants in late October, it all looks a tad Communist State. Apart from the odd beetroot, you'll find yourself staring at a literal waste of space.

But fear not, overwintering vegetables are at hand. Specifically, leeks, onions, shallots and garlic (see pages 138 and 144); aka The Saviours of Winter. They don't just survive growing over the winter months – they prefer it, the hardy renegades. Planted in autumn when the vegetable patch is forlornly empty, this unlikely band of heroes will grow away while you hibernate and be ready to pick the next summer. Winter vegetable woes SORTED.

Just one thing . . . prepare yourself to think carefully about timings. The earliest that any of your veg will be ready is May – a month after we all need to plant spring's earliest seedlings. The latest is July, when the whole veg plot is in full swing. I predict a riot. Plan ahead before you fill every bed in sight or there'll be nowhere to plant your new-season crops. I happily planted my spring plants in between the onions, shallots and garlic this year (I'd deliberately left room between rows) and bar a few scuffles, they all got along famously.

SOIL

Here's the truth about soil . . . it doesn't really matter what kind you have. (A million gardeners gasp.) As ever, nothing is truly insurmountable. Particularly for us and our small gardens, because much of what we're planting will be growing in newly created pots, planters and raised beds (compost-filled, manure- and fertiliser-enriched, beautifully draining). However, if, like me, you have a nice big flowerbed or two, there's still nothing to lose sleep over.

The biggest thing to think about is drainage – you basically want not too little, not too much. After a heavy downpour, go outside and have a look at your soil. If you have puddles hanging about for ages afterwards, you've probably got heavy, slow-draining soil. Break it up with a fork, dig in some mulch/bark/compost and add a bit of gravel or horticultural sand. This will vastly improve both the drainage and nutrient content, ready for planting. If you notice that your soil's dry and 'sandy' textured, again, dig in mulch/compost but leave out the gravel and sand. In fact, whatever the soil problem, the answer is usually to dig in some mulch/compost. It's like magic.

Keep your eye out for specific recommendations through the book, such as digging in well-rotted manure the autumn before for particularly hungry plants, adding bonemeal to keep roses happy and using potting compost for container plants. Peat-free compost is also a must when selecting a big bag for your bed. We don't want to go wrecking the environment in the process of improving our own patches.

GROWING UP

If, like me, you have a small garden, you'll rapidly find yourself running out of growing space once your gardening obsession takes hold. So . . . what do you do when you run out of space on the floor? You start growing upwards, that's what. Right up the walls and fences.

CLIMBERS

Climbing, quick-growing evergreen plants, such as jasmine (see page 239) and rambling roses (see page 220), are perfect for disguising knackered old fences and boring expanses of wall. Try throwing in a bit of honeysuckle (see page 242) or clematis for good measure – they'll magically make your garden smell like a posh perfume department in spring and summer, but they will also make it look like it's been there for a long time. Established. Like the sort of thing you see in your mum's *Homes & Gardens* magazine. *She says, hiding her copy*.

Handy hint: A note on supporting climbers. Perhaps unsurprisingly, your climbing plants will need something to climb up. Stretching lengths of wire along your fence or wall horizontally, at intervals, is the answer. Fixing a trellis to the top of a fence will add height and support, too.

A SORT-OF LIVING WALL

Is there anything trendier than a living wall? No. Not even Beyoncé in a self-designed sports label. Take a walk through any capital city from New York to Stockholm and there they'll be. In fancy clothing stores, at the entrance to Michelin-starred restaurants, covering the walls of upmarket hotel chains. Beautiful, in their ferny, frondy lusciousness.

However, professionally designed and installed living walls are what my grandma would have called 'ruinously expensive'. There are some vertical growing kits you can buy online (though I've found it hard to find any that look nice), and you could go down the pallet-hack route, but personally, I've decided to take inspiration from a more old-fashioned place . . . Cornwall. More specifically, the lovely old walls in Cornwall's famous winding lanes, ancient barns and creekside jetties.

Wherever you look, one thing's the same . . . carpets of flowers, ferns, succulents and moss growing across their surface. In particular you'll see Cornish daisies – those little white and pink flowers poking their heads out of even the dankest and dreariest wall. (Cornish daisies are actually called Mexican Fleabane, by the way. No wonder it took me so bloody long to find them.) Perfect for shadowy walls and easily ordered online. Similarly, *Saxifraga* x *urbium*, with its tiny white flowers, is an excellent choice. Apologies for the Latin, but this is the best way to find it in a Google search. Its more common name is, in fact, London Pride – so-called because of its resilience during the Blitz. Springing up on bombsites, it became a symbol of hope to Londoners. What better plant to grow in a city garden? Add a selection of succulents and ferns to the cracks in your wall and you have the makings of a fine living wall.

Planting them is easy. Simply remove any weeds in the space where you want them to grow, then press small seedlings into the cracks with a little compost. Seeds work well too – just mix them with the compost, pack it into the cracks and away you go. I've also planted some of these flowers in pots at the bottom of the wall to encourage future seeds to spread into any areas I can't reach. Helpfully, these flowers have very shallow roots so they won't damage your wall either.

Moss makes a great finishing touch to a living wall. Remarkably, all you need to do is collect some, break it into small pieces, remove as much dirt from the roots as possible, then blend it with natural yoghurt, water and half a teaspoon of sugar. Then take your mixture and paint it on with a paintbrush. No one saw that coming.

GARDEN DESIGN

On its most basic level, the grand term 'garden design' can be described as 'making your garden feel like yours'. A garden is a wonderful thing, no matter how small it is. A space where you can escape to and be your daft, unguarded sef.

The scale of design can be as ambitious as you like. In a rented flat, you're hardly going to spend thousands of pounds on a total redesign with expensive reclaimed flagstones, but a colourful table and chairs, a bright umbrella and wrapping the trunk of a tree in twinkly lights? Totally doable. Buy a few bright pink plastic flamingos, string up the bunting, procure a length of French café-style festoon lighting and fire up the BBQ. Garden party heaven. Basically, if you like it, it's right. There are no stern rules to follow here. Which is lucky, as I've just this week hung a sparkly disco ball from the balcony.

If, on the other hand, you're lucky enough to own your space, get the DIY box out – we're going to build a raised bed (see page 48).

The aim is thus: create a garden in which you can chill out, potter about, invite your friends round and get totally gazebo'd. Here are some ideas you might like to try.

ALL THE COLOURS

Working as a creative director, it was once suggested that my favourite colour was 'all of them'. It's true. I'm an unrestrained rainbow unicorn where colour is concerned.

I love colour in a garden. I like mine to feel silly and joyful and fun. Let loose your inner crazed Karl Lagerfeld. Paint that random metal pillar pink. It's easy to underestimate the power of a few good sploshes of bright colour shining out against all the green that nature provides.

These days, DIY emporiums stock all sorts of shades in their outdoor paint aisle. You can even get the embarrassed teenage Saturday lad to mix bespoke colours for you at the bigger outlets, so if you fancy painting a wall the exact blue of Yves Saint Lauren's Moroccan garden, you can now recreate it in Surbiton. Wood, metal, concrete . . . there's a paint for any surface you fancy attacking with a paintbrush. In my garden I turned the rusty old pillars under upstairs' balcony candyfloss pink, much to Timmy's dismay. On a smaller scale, painting a normal brown garden pot with an outlandish colour adds an instant 'where did you get that, Selfridges?' quality to it.

Handy hint: White fences. In a small garden, painting your fences white works a treat. Not only does it boost light levels for your plants (and you, tanning in your deckchair), but it also makes the area look bigger.

HIGHS AND LOWS

Vary heights. That's my advice to you. Varying the heights of plants in your garden will add depth and interest and, strangely, make your garden look bigger, disguising the edges and pulling the eye to the centre. The aim is to hide where your garden boundary begins and ends. It's an evolving process, so there's no need to worry about getting it right straight away. As time goes on, you might want to fill a bald-looking spot with a new plant – plug these with annual flowers for the season and tinker as your plants mature.

Just remember: tall plants at the back, short ones at the front. Don't laugh. I made that mistake once. There were tears . . .

We've covered climbers already (see page 40), but getting some big, medium-height, structural 'fillers' into any beds or large containers will do wonders for breaking up hard lines. Pop down to your garden centre and have a rummage. There are endless evergreen options in the shrub section, for all soil and light conditions.

There's also the option of hanging plants. I picked up some colourful little buckets which are ingeniously designed to hook over a fence or balcony rail. I've planted all sorts in them over the years, from edible flowers to trailing ivy. Securing coloured pots in a pattern across a wall is an excellent way to add interest and increase growing space. Alternatively, may I tempt you to a vintage hanging birdcage? Fill it with succulents and trailing ivy and you'll have a beautiful, unusual feature.

Handy hint: Heavenly bamboo (or *Nandina domestica*, as some garden centres insist on calling it) is the very best bush I've ever purchased. Fast-growing, space-filling, full of colour all year round, his leaves start purple, turn light green to dark, then return to a reddish-purple come winter. He grows lovely white bee-friendly flowers, followed by red berries. And he's a hardy little bugger. Happy in any soil, just pop him in a sunny sheltered spot and remember to water him in dry spells. Reaching a maximum height and spread of 1.5 x 1.5m, he's great for filling out a new bed. Not bad for £15.

ALTERNATIVE POTS AND PLANTERS

Use that imagination of yours. Does your local takeaway chuck out really cool-looking oil drums with bright Indian lettering all over them? After a good wash, this is courgette heaven in the making. Do you have a big off-licence or wine warehouse near you? Ask if you can squirrel away one or two empty wooden wine crates. Drill holes in the bottom and, lo, you've created the perfect snuggly strawberry home (see page 176). Lucky strawberries.

Milk churns. Old barrels. Boring plastic pots painted bright colours with exterior-paint tester pots. I once saw Kirstie Allsopp dive into a skip on national television on the hunt for such things. Sod it . . . do like Kirstie Allsopp. Go shamelessly foraging for other people's tat, then transform it in your garden. You'll be the king of Pinterest before you know it.

Handy hint: Here's a helpful tip for you when planting in pots. When filling your containers, large or small, put a layer of stones/bits of old brick/broken pots/whatever you find lying around in the bottom. This will help water drain out of the pot (so long as there are holes in the bottom – make sure to drill some if there aren't any), rather than collecting around the plant roots and drowning them.

HOW TO PAINT A BITCHIN' BIRDHOUSE

Ain't nothin' cooler than a bright pink birdhouse. Only . . . well, a £9.99 bog-standard FSC wooden birdhouse isn't pink. It's brown. Perfectly nice, but not the gaudy colour I was hoping for. The solution . . .? Exterior wood paint, of course.

A full 2.5-litre can seemed a bit excessive (and expensive), but then I spied a row of tiny tester pots. I bought three pots but, would you believe it, I managed to do the whole thing with just one. It's a painty miracle. One nice thick layer, left to dry in the sun, then repeated to even out the colour. It's the campest birdhouse in all of London.

OUTDOOR SHELVES

If all you have is a vast, flat, vertical wall to work with, drill some shelves into it. Genius. From nowhere for pots and planters to sit, to all the surface area you could hope for.

Alternatively, try a fancy garden shelf ladder. No drilling required; simply lean it against your wall and fill with planters. Wooden wine crates, old pots, brightly coloured tin buckets. The world is your oyster.

Handy hint: All hail the BBQ. It's basically illegal to have a garden without a BBQ, so work out where you're going to put yours. On our tiny rented balcony we had two dedicated bricks on which to perch the disposable tin-foil version (we knew how to live). Nowadays, we have a genuinely fancy Weber – but it took me years to save up for this sort of outlandish fire-making, so go with whatever you can afford. On a sunny day, it really doesn't matter what you cook on – charred sausages and a pitcher of disastrously strong Pimm's will outdo any restaurant in the *Michelin Guide*.

HOW TO BUILD A RAISED BED

This is by far the biggest, most ambitious project in this book, but it's also the most useful and rewarding on the 'Mum, look what I made' scale. I desperately wanted a proper space to grow vegetables, despite our tiny garden, and this was the ultimate solution.

However, it turns out that building a raised bed involves an enormous amount of effort, splinters and forward thinking (snore). Here's the most important thing you need to build a raised bed: friends. Bribe them with beer. Lure them with lunch. Then work them like a chain gang. So, how do you build a raised bed?

Here's what you'll need:

Makes a 4m x 60cm long narrow raised bed, 3 planks high

7 x 4m scaffold planks, 1 plank cut into 6 x 60cm lengths

12 x 90cm lengths of treated 2 x 2 wood

12 x 10mm coach bolts, plus nuts to fit

72 x 8mm screws

A power drill with selection of drill bits and screwdriver attachment

A circular saw (you can hire these)

N.B. For a smaller or bigger bed, simply change the plank lengths to fit your space – the method stays the same.

1. MEASURE: First, decide how big you want it (in our case, a massive 4 metres long, nearly all the way down one side of our garden) and how wide (60cm – so we could easily reach over to the other side without having to climb into it).

2. PICK WOODEN PLANKS: I wanted a faded, beachy, solid/thick feel – as inexpensive as possible – and after a lot of research opted for reclaimed scaffolding boards. Discovered on Google, delivered from the Midlands. If you have a lot of room, massive great railway sleepers look wonderful and will survive even a meteor strike. Alternatively, try using treated wooden planks from a timber yard or DIY store. You can even lay bricks (though I'd advise getting this done professionally).

3. CLEAR AREA: Strip back any grass, pebbles, flagstones or any other sort of covering in the area where you want to build, levelling off the ground with a spade. We marked out the area with string, staked into the ground with canes.

4. CUT TO SIZE: Once you have the planks, hire a circular saw to cut through them – this was proper scary, so I made Tim do it. In fact, this is the most dangerous power tool we've ever used, so get your most capable friend or relative to help, following every single safety instruction to the letter. Alternatively, get a lumber yard or big DIY store to cut your wood to length.

5. BUILD THE FRAME: If you're building a tall raised bed you'll need to make four solid 'walls' from your planks. The planks need to be strongly fixed together and flush so the soil doesn't escape between the gaps. Ratchet straps (the kind you get to secure things to car roofs) will help secure them as you work – affix one at each end and one in the middle of each 'wall', tightened as tight as they can to force the planks into a perfect, solid, gap-free structure.

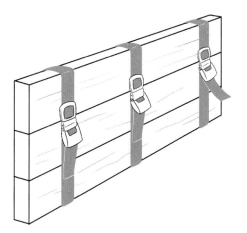 

Next, position your 2 x 2 pieces vertically against the two longest horizontal plank walls – one at each end and the rest evenly spaced along its length. The top should be flush with the top of the planks, the other end will poke out beneath – these are the legs that will fix the bed into the ground. Screw in place the 2 x 2s using two screws per plank, one at the top and one at the bottom – drill guide holes first with a drill bit 1–2mm smaller than your screw diameter. Repeat with the other three scaffold planks. You now have two long sides. For the short sides, repeat the steps above, but only fix a single vertical 2 x 2 in the middle of each plank to add support instead of at each end.

Next, get some help and flip the four sides up onto their legs. It's time to fix it together with coach bolts. Drill a hole the size of the bolt through the end of one short side and through the 2 x 2 on the long side to attach the two pieces at a right angle. Insert the bolt and tighten to make a solid soil-proof seal. Repeat for each end plank, twelve times in all. Flip the bed over so it's standing on its legs. Then dig little holes and sink the legs into them. Check the bed is level and backfill with soil around the legs to secure them into place.

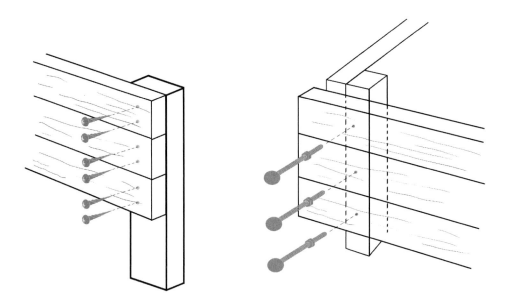

6. FILL BED: Once you've finished your frame, congratulate yourself profusely. After that, it's time to fill it. That's right, more hard labour. Cue two tonnes of topsoil arriving at our doorstep (again, another Google search for the best price). That's a LOT of lugging soil. When the bed is almost full, dig in three big sacks of manure then two big sacks of compost so it is all rich and nutritious for your plants. Then suddenly, before you know it, your raised bed is finished! Resplendent, beautiful and ready for planting.

I'll be honest . . . it's the most exciting, satisfying, constructive thing I've done in a long time. Sure, the effort nearly broke us, but it's now one of the major features in our garden, has weathered beautifully and year after year has produced an astonishing amount of produce. All hail the raised bed.

Handy hint: The best time to do any of the big stuff, such as fence mending, painting or constructing raised beds, is in late autumn and winter, when there's nothing much growing. Sling on a bobble hat and some old jeans, put some rum in that mug of coffee and start to turn your genius garden plan into reality, laughing an evil laugh as you go.

INTRODUCING THE PUB SHED

If you have enough room, a shed is an investment that won't let you down. You see, the more over-excited you become on the gardening front, the more 'stuff' you'll buy. Tools, deckchairs, bags of compost, pots, shears, umbrellas, garden canes. It's bamboozling. However, you can also use your shed as a canvas upon which to unleash that dastardly imagination of yours. Painting a shed adds a brilliant big area of colour and jaunty seaside feel to even the most landlocked of back yards.

But why stop at a purely functional piece of garden storage when you can make it into your own tiny pub? Yes, the pub shed. 'Tis a thing of great beauty and wonder.

I bought one for Tim as a Christmas present – the smallest shed you can buy with a window, measuring 6 x 4 feet. Man, Timmy loves his shed. What makes it a pub? This is the exciting bit. We carefully removed the glass (by unscrewing one side of the wooden mount so that we could slide it out whenever we need to) to create a serving hatch. Then Timmy manfully and impressively sawed a thick piece of wood (an offcut from our raised bed) to the length of the window. He added cheap wooden shelf brackets to support its weight, and a bar top was born, right under the inside of the window.

To finish, get on the eBay, snuffle about in a junk shop or visit a big antiques fair. You'll find everything from optics (to hold your bottles of spirit), to old pub signs, to a salvaged hand beer pump. Buy a little barrel of beer from your local brewery and find a sheet of those naked lady peanuts for the back of the door for a real sense of kitsch authenticity. We even made a back bar out of an old crate for all of our booze bottles.

Pub shed DONE. Friends and family beside themselves with jealousy.

Handy hint: Look for the FSC stamp of approval when choosing your wooden shed. It guarantees that the timber comes from a sustainably sourced and managed woodland, meaning you can sleep at night instead of slowly weeping under the burden of environmental guilt.

Right. Enough of the preamble. Let's get gardening.

HERBS

HERBS

The fact is, herbs are so easy to grow that they don't need pages and pages of explanation. As Tim has just said over my shoulder, 'Herbs? Just stick them in a pot and let them get on with it.' The master hath spoken.

However, they're an excellent and fancy-looking windowsill addition, no matter where you live: a perfect place to start our growing adventures. Whether you have a sunny windowsill, small garden or tiny patio space, creating a little plant-pot herb garden is a great way to grow these kitchen essentials.

On our first balcony we had a whole mish-mash of herbs in two long containers, but after a while they started to bully each other. The sage crowded out the lemon thyme. The rosemary went feral and killed the mint. It was carnage. So forever more I shall keep them in quarantine, in separate pots.

Over the years I've tried growing all sorts of herbs, but what follows are the old dependables, all available as seedlings from the garden centre in spring, easy to grow and arguably the most useful in your day-to-day cooking.

INSIDE OR OUTSIDE

Bar the bay tree, all of the following can happily live indoors if they have one key thing: a sunny window to sit by. Indoor herbs need at least 4–6 hours of direct sunlight each day to flourish.

Then it's very simple. Plant your herbs in as big a pot as your windowsill/kitchen counter/office desk will happily take, with adequate drainage (holes in the bottom of the container, rocks/pebbles in the bottom), filled with potting soil and watered regularly enough not to dry out but not so often that the soil becomes soggy.

Handy hint: Because they're not going to get rained on, you have a lot more options for ingenious and stylish containers if you're keeping your herbs inside (rust not being a problem). Classic Colman's mustard tins make beautiful pots, as do golden syrup tins.

THE BIG HERB HARVESTING RULE

Whether you're growing them inside or out, don't pick all of your herbs' big leaves. It seems obvious now I'm writing it, but the number of times I've got a bit over-enthusiastic and nearly finished off the basil . . .

Those big tasty leaves are your herbs' power stations. Try to take a mixture of small new leaves and big older ones when you go picking. You'll find you have a healthier, happier, far more leafy plant for longer.

Aside from that, it's best to harvest your herbs in the early morning, when their essential oils are at their most abundant. Who knew?

CHIVES

[PERENNIAL]

| Seeds | March–June | Full sun | Grows to fill container | July– September |

Chives are surprisingly easy to grow, look lovely with their edible purple flowers, will return year after year once planted and, most importantly of all, taste freakin' delicious. Adding a light, delicate oniony flavour to everything from potato salads to omelettes to salmon blini starters, you can eat the stalk and the flower.

To grow, scatter your chive seeds lightly across the surface of a container (at least 15cm wide) filled with potting compost and cover with a thin layer of soil. Keep the soil moist and cut the chives with scissors as needed, leaving 5cm at the base to ensure they keep growing. After dying back in winter, your chives will return the next spring.

LEMON THYME

[PERENNIAL]

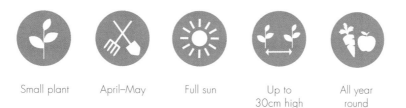

Small plant   April–May   Full sun   Up to 30cm high   All year round

The more exciting member of the thyme family, you may not be surprised to hear that lemon thyme adds a lovely subtle, lemony note to dishes and is particularly tasty with roast chicken. Lemon thyme also has beautiful leaves and will make an attractive 30cm-high bush in a bed if you have any gaps that need filling.

Lemon thyme will live very happily in a big pot, too. Tough and drought resistant, he's happiest in direct sun, hates being waterlogged (herbs really do hate soggy roots) and should be cut back hard, regularly, even if it grows faster than you can eat it, to stop it becoming leggy.

BAY TREE

[PERENNIAL]

Small plant   April–September   Full sun/part shade   Up to 15m tall   All year round

The bay tree isn't a seedling, he's a tree, and consequently lives in the biggest container you own. Plant in soil-based compost with extra grit added to improve stability and drainage. Bay is a wonderfully flexible fellow; you can use bay leaves fresh or dried, and they are particularly good in slow-cooked winter stews.

A bay tree is very easy to look after. Feed with tomato feed every two weeks from mid-spring to late summer. If there's going to be a hard frost, wrap some fleece around the pot. Don't over-water in summer. Re-pot every 2–3 years in spring and trim his branches in the summer with secateurs to maintain a nice shape. Happy bay trees all round.

MINT

[PERENNIAL]

| Small plant | April–September | Full sun/partial shade | Will grow to fill container | March–October |

I have a mint tea obsession, so growing mint myself is essential to ensuring I'm not ruined financially. Aunty Jan says mint is a rampant rogue that shouldn't be planted in a bed lest it take over the entire garden (hence why some people sink pots into their flowerbed so as to contain its roots). Me? I've taken a more devil-may-care approach: I had a bald patch to fill, and a mint habit to fuel. Win-win.

When your mint's finished flowering in late summer, cut him back to 5cm above soil level and wait for his return next spring. Hooray for mint.

BASIL

[ANNUAL]

| Small plant | May–July | Full sun | Will grow to fill container | May–September |

Basil is an Italian show pony. He only likes the heat and sunshine and insists on a regular sprinkle under the hose before dying as soon as it's autumn. But you know what? It's dead tasty, and even supermarket basil can become a prolific grower throughout spring and summer if planted outside.

About six weeks after planting out, pinch out the bud on top of the centre stem to encourage more stems to grow at the side so that the plant becomes bushy. Pick leaves regularly and he'll keep on growing more, particularly if you take them from the top of the plant.

Handy hint: Only water basil in the morning. He hates going to bed with wet roots.

ROSEMARY

[PERENNIAL]

| Small plant | May– September | Full sun/ part shade | Will grow to fill container | All year round |

Remarkably, I've never managed to kill Mr Rosemary. Not only is he endlessly useful in the kitchen, he's Bruce Willis levels of tough, too. Try to remember to water him in hot spells. When he's finished flowering, feed him with fertiliser and then carefully cut off all his branches close to the main stem with scissors to allow him to grow back next year. Done.

If he's outside and you're being particularly kind, raise his pot off the ground in winter, or tuck him in with a layer of mulch if he's planted in a bed. Some people add horticultural fleece to the branches in hard frost. I wish I could say I'd ever remembered to do this. Let's hope you treat your rosemary better.

SAGE

[PERENNIAL]

| Small plant | May– September | Full sun/ part shade | Will grow to fill container | All year round |

Have you ever tried fried sage with butter in pasta (burro e salvia, if we're getting Italian)? It's worth growing sage for this dish alone. Mr Sage insists on a good regular watering, especially in a heatwave and preferably in the morning (herbs hate having wet roots when they're sleeping. Understandable, I'd be uncomfortable, too). Cut your sage back to a few inches above the soil after flowering and he'll be a happy little fellow.

Sage prefers a sheltered spot, out of direct sun and strong wind. If growing in a pot, make sure it's at least 45cm in diameter. If growing in a bed, fork in some well-rotted manure to help him on his way.

VEG
ETA
BLES

VEGETABLES

Vegetables. The main reason I embarked upon this whole 'growing stuff' malarkey in the first place. As anyone who knows me will attest, I love food. Cooking food. Eating food. Feeling up tomatoes daaaaaan the market like some sort of heirloom pervert. So to be able to grow vegetables myself, despite not owning a farm, was somewhat of a revelation.

To me, there's something outrageously opulent about stepping out into the garden and pottering back into the kitchen, victorious, holding genuine free food aloft, ready to cook then and there. On a school night.

Alongside the joy of tomatoes that actually taste of tomato, and tiny potatoes dug from the earth with your own two hands, is the equally exciting prospect of growing vegetables that are both hard to find and expensive to buy once you track them down. Fresh horseradish root. Dinky sweet yellow courgettes.

Fresher. Tastier. Perfectly imperfect in appearance. The following vegetables are easy to grow, and more flavourful than anything you'll find in a supermarket. Happiness, found in a tiny plot of soil.

CARROTS

[ANNUAL]

| Seedlings | March–June | Full sun/ part shade | 10cm apart | May– November |

Due to a rare quirk in my DNA, I am only capable of growing wonky carrots. However, genetic flaws aside, Chantenay carrots – triangular little fellas who don't grow more than 12cm long – are genuinely properly difficult to mess up, so perfect for both pots and beginners alike.

The following guidence will also work for little round Atlas carrots (I say round, but, again, mine turned out like wonky little freak crabs. Stop laughing. It's genetic) and bog-standard 'carrots' from the garden centre.

So, carrots ahoy. Let's get going.

TO PLANT

WHEN: I plant mine at the end of March if it's a nice spring and I'm getting over-excited, but April onwards as a general, more self-controlled rule.

WHERE: Carrots like natural light, but not an overly sunny spot.

HOW: Water the ground well, then dig in a little compost or well-rotted manure (they don't need much – a sprinkle should do it). Then make a small hole for each plant – the same size as the ball of soil your seedling's roots are contained within. And that's it. A few slug pellets scattered around, and your carrots are ready to carrot.

Handy hint: Make sure you separate and plant every single tiny seedling individually. Carrot seedlings sometimes come grown in 'clusters' within the separate pods of a plastic tray. A mistake I made the first time I tried to grow them. Things got inappropriately cosy.

SPACE: Plant your seedlings about 10cm away from each other, with 30cm between rows if you're going carrot crazy

Good news, carrot fans; carrots are just as happy growing in containers as they are in the ground. Choose a shorter variety and a container at least 20cm deep, then fill it up with compost and plant as above. Something to try: If you have a tall chimney pot or milk-can-style planter, toy with a longer carrot variety. I'm trying this at the moment and, if Tim's granddad is to be believed, this should encourage really straight carrots. Let me know how yours work out.

KEEPING THEM ALIVE

You'll need to feed your carrot friends throughout the season. I use a sprinkle of tomato feed every two weeks. Carrots are pretty unassuming characters, but they do insist that their soil doesn't dry out, especially during hot weather, so keep them watered.

HARVESTING

WHEN: Gently feel around just under the soil surface with your fingers. When your carrots reach 2–3cm in diameter they're ready to pick. If they still have a little way to go, cover them up and let them get back to growing.

HOW: Carrots are easy to harvest; simply hold on tightly to the bundle of stalks, close to the soil surface, and pull them up. Done.

Handy hint: Water the soil before pulling up carrots. They'll come up far easier, with less root breakage and disturbance which means they won't emit their seductive carrot fly-attracting aroma (see below).

HOW OFTEN: I pick them as I need them/as they reach full size. You can always take some smaller ones early then leave the rest to reach their fullest carroty size.

POTENTIAL DISASTERS

Carrot fly is whispered quietly on allotments across the land. Their larvae are truly Machiavellian little wankers who feed on the roots of the carrot, then tunnel into the developing veg, causing it to rot. And the worst part? There's nothing you can do if it happens. So it's all about prevention. Be careful not to break leaves when thinning (so as not to release that carrot-fly-attracting smell). Water the soil before picking to prevent root damage as you pull them up, and if you're very worried, you can construct cunning 20–30cm-high vertical barriers of polythene around them to keep the low-flying female flies out.

Green carrots, or the green tops of the carrot, to be more accurate, happen when they're accidentally exposed to sun during growing. Heavy rain can wash away soil, exposing their bald little heads. Get in there and tuck them back in again. Orange carrots once more. Sorted.

FROM THE GARDEN TO THE TABLE

SAVOURY CARROT TARTE TATIN

Serves 4 as a lunch with salad

Those cheeky French, holding back on us all these years. There we all were, thinking that tarte Tatin was an apple-based dessert, when for centuries our Gallic cousins have been Tatining the hell out of everything in sight, including 'les légumes' (GCSE French still going strong). I once had a slice of caramelised onion tarte Tatin so tasty that I nearly cried when I finished it. But that's Parisian cafés for you. They're very emotional. Today we're using carrots. Picked straight from our garden, washed, and caramelised to perfection in this kitchen garden classic.

Here's what you'll need:

35g salted butter

8–10 medium carrots, halved lengthways (enough to tightly pack in as one layer in the pan)

3 thyme sprigs

170ml freshly squeezed carrot juice (or orange juice)

250g puff pastry

1 tbsp red wine vinegar

A good pinch of sea salt

A few big cracks of black pepper

1 tbsp runny honey

1 tbsp pomegranate syrup (or honey)

Preheat the oven to 180°C/350°F/gas 4.

In a frying pan, melt the butter until it starts to foam. Chuck in the carrots and thyme, giving the carrots a good shuffle until they're coated evenly in the butter–thyme mixture. After 6–7 minutes, add the carrot juice, pop a lid on and cook for 7–8 minutes, tossing them now and then so they don't burn.

While the carrots are cooking, cut out the pastry. On a clean work surface, roll the pastry to roughly ½cm thick, then place your pan upside-down in the middle of the pastry. I cut about 1cm bigger than the pan as puff pastry shrinks a little during baking. Set aside.

Back to the carrots. At the very last minute, drain them, then add the vinegar, salt and pepper and shuffle them all about so that everything's coated.

Now for the tatining. In the bottom of your Tatin pan, drizzle the honey and pomegranate syrup then swirl to coat the surface evenly. Carefully arrange your carrots in the pan, packing them in as tightly as is humanly possible, to create a solid layer of carroty wonder. Remember, this will be the top of your tart. If ever there's been a time for spoddy neatness, it's now. Season with salt and pepper, if you like, then carefully lay the pastry over them, tucking in the edges.

Use a 24cm ovenproof tall-sided frying pan, or similar (it keeps all the juices in) or a tarte Tatin dish

IMPORTANT NOTE: Cooking the perfect tarte tatin is not as easy as cookbooks would have you believe. The problem is you can't see what the carrots are doing under that there pastry. It will take 30–35 minutes for the pastry to puff up to golden perfection, but peek through the oven door periodically. Are the carrots catching? If so, take them out. Don't worry if it goes a little awry on the first try, this always tastes amazing – it's just the 'look' that takes a little practice.

Take the pan out of the oven with an oven glove or thick folded towel, then place a serving dish on top and carefully flip the tart. It should come away easily. In case of tatin emergency, gently slip a flat-bladed knife around the edge to unstick the pastry.

Serve straight away with a big salad (grown in your garden, perhaps? See page 144) and French vinaigrette. The perfect lunch.

CARROT GREENS CHIMICHURRI

Makes 1 big mugful

Did you know that you can eat the stalks and leaves of carrots – the carrot tops? Neither did I! Not until researching this very chapter. All these years of throwing them away . . . Well, not any more. It turns out, carrot tops are flippin' tasty.

You can blitz them into a pesto instead of basil, but we've got a nasturtium pesto recipe coming up later (see page 218), so we're going Argentinean instead. 'Chimichurri' – as good to say as it is to eat. Drizzle it on everything in sight (particularly meat and fish) or use it as a dip for their roasted carrot chums.

Here's what you'll need:

A great big handful of carrot greens, finely chopped

2 tsp dried oregano

2 tsp ground sweet paprika

¼ tsp ground cumin

2 dried red chillies, flaked

120ml white wine vinegar

120ml really good-quality extra virgin olive oil

A few cracks of freshly ground black pepper

A good sprinkle of crushed sea salt

This one's very simple. Pop all the ingredients in a bowl and mix it all up. Ta da!

HORSERADISH

[PERENNIAL]

Young plant   March–May   Part shade   1m apart   November–February

Glimpse an early photo of me and my enormous horseradish plant and you'd never know that The Great Slug Ravaging happened . . . Or The Great Caterpillar Ravaging. Or 'The Time I Accidentally Fell Onto It When I Was Drunk In The Garden'. The horseradish, truly, is the Rocky of the Brassicaceae family.

Fresh horseradish is a thing of beauty. Forget everything you know about the processed, watered-down stuff you buy in jars – a fresh grating of horseradish root gives the sort of clean, bright peppery punch that causes an involuntary wince/cry/brain-cringe/'fook me' reaction. Which is a splendid thing. Honest.

Handy hint: Taste aside, horseradish is extremely helpful if you're growing potatoes, increasing disease resistance and keeping away pests such as the Colorado beetle. (They can't hack his wasabi smell.)

TO PLANT

WHEN: You'll find young plants in the veg section of larger garden centres or online from early March. The short planting season of March–May ensures the plants take root before the weather gets too hot.

WHERE: In my garden, there's a really annoying shady end of my raised bed, and because it's far from the back door it's often forgotten in a busy week. Perfect conditions for horseradish. Why? Because neglect it all you like, horseradish will merrily potter away on its own, perfectly happy. Bless it. Think about where to plant before you dig him in – you don't want to move this perennial once in the ground.

HOW: There are two tactics for planting horseradish. One: dig a hole and pop your plant straight into the soil, watering thoroughly. Or, as horseradish can get seriously over-excited and spread well beyond its remit, two: the 'bottomless pot' technique. Get a large plastic flowerpot, cut off the bottom and sink this into the bed, then plant the horseradish in the middle. Clever.

SPACE: I wouldn't advise growing more than one plant, as they get so big and make so many edible roots, but if you're a horseradish fundamentalist, make sure each plant is at least 1m away from its neighbour.

Without a stern talking to horseradish can get out of hand. For this reason, many gardeners prefer to plant these fiery renegades in containers. The bigger the pot, the better. Horseradish needs at least a 30cm depth, but 50cm or more will give it room to grow bigger, fatter, longer roots.

KEEPING THEM ALIVE

I'll be genuinely surprised if you manage to kill your horseradish. It's almost Steven Segal tough.

That said, there are a few things that can seriously piss off a horseradish. If your soil becomes absolutely waterlogged, as in a sustained flood, it could die. Though mine is in a shady spot, it does get a little bit of sun in the early morning. Absolute darkness might tip it over the edge.

But other than that . . . it's a case of holding the old rogue back. After much research, my highly technical summary is thus: hack it back whenever it starts to get too much. No matter how much you cut the leaves or how much root you harvest (as long as you leave one tiny piece) it will survive.

HARVESTING

WHEN: Ok. This isn't going to be easy for the impatient amongst you (me). You have to wait at least one year before harvesting your first horseradish root. I know. What the . . .? But trust me on this. Give it a chance to establish and it will give you a tasty harvest every year forever and ever.

After that, the rules are simple. Wait for the first frost (November at the earliest) then go for your life – this is when the flavour is most intense.

HOW: Get a nice big digging fork and loosen the soil around the plant. Then switch to the two spades on the end of your arms, otherwise known as hands. Poke around with your fingers and find the direction in which your crazy horseradish root has grown. Unlike other roots, a horseradish's main root will be found running nearly horizontal in a completely random direction. Once you've found it, follow it with your fork, carefully removing the soil around it.

Rummaging around like this means not only will you get the largest roots, which easily snap off if you pull them, but you'll lessen the chance of accidentally leaving small pieces of root in the ground. This is bad. Every tiny piece of root left behind can turn into a whole new plant. And that means . . . Horseradish Apocalypse. If you do see unwanted plants springing up in the summer, carefully uproot them using this 'fork and finger' method. Panic over. Stand down.

Ooh, and one more thing. Don't peel your horseradish straight away. Trim and wash the roots, pat dry with a tea towel and seal in a plastic bag or airtight container in the fridge until needed. They will last for several weeks.

HOW OFTEN: A few times throughout the winter, as soon as you need new fresh roots. I seem to return 3–4 times in a season.

POTENTIAL DISASTERS

I stand by it. If you manage to fudge up your horseradish, hats off to your jam-fool self. I'd like a photo of you and your gardening fingertips of doom. If you're very unlucky, **club root** can strike, which is a fungal infection that causes the root to go all Elephant Man. It's rare in horseradish, but the good news is . . . you could still eat the roots even if they do come out wonky.

Handy hint: Pests will continually try to have a go at your horseradish leaves, but in the long run, they won't do much harm. Caterpillars, in particular, seem to view it much like The Cookie Monster views, well, cookies. You can pick caterpillars off by hand *squeals like a tiny girl for a moment* or just ignore them. Similarly with flies. Mostly, I just let them get on with it, or else reach for Timmy's trusty magic pest-killing formula (see page 30) and give them a good squirt.

FROM THE GARDEN TO THE TABLE:

THE ULTIMATE FRESH HORSERADISH SAUCE

Makes a ramekin dish of sauce

Here's what you'll need:

1 x 20–25cm piece of horseradish root, grated

1 tbsp white wine vinegar

A pinch of sea salt

1 tbsp water

2 tbsp double cream/natural yoghurt/crème fraîche/sour cream

Freshly ground black pepper

If you've got this far into this horseradish section, I'm assuming you like horseradish. Perhaps you're the one who asks for a second pot of horseradish with your roast at the pub and, deep down, is only into sushi because of the wasabi? Yes? Then these recipes are for you, my brain-wincing sadist friend. The process for making horseradish is easy. The hard part? Choosing which tasty creamy ingredient to make it with:

Double cream: Rich, French, amazing with slow-cooked beef or a pan-fried steak. You can whip it for a lighter texture, or keep it thin and drizzle it straight over your meat.

Crème fraîche: A lighter alternative to double cream, which I usually opt for. Slightly tangy, slightly nutty, all the horseradish oomph without the nagging creamy guilt.

Natural yoghurt: Similar to crème fraîche, but can only be used with cold dishes (hello fancy roast beef sandwich). If put with a hot dish, the yoghurt will split or curdle.

Sour cream: Particularly good with potato latkes and salmon (see page 90). I often add a squeeze of lemon, too. Like yoghurt, sour cream should only be used with cold dishes.

Rinse and peel the freshly picked horseradish root with a potato peeler. (Brace yourself; it can be pretty darned punchy. I usually prepare mine outside, even if it's raining.) Then either grate it with a fine cheese grater, or, if you're lucky enough to have a food processor, cut the root into chunks and blitz the lot.

Mix the horseradish with the vinegar and salt, adding a little water as you go, until you've created a smooth paste that isn't too watery. At this stage, you can pop it in a sterile, airtight jar where it will keep quite happily for 3–4 weeks in the fridge.

Once you've prepared the horseradish, take 2 tablespoons of the horseradish mixture and add it to 2 tablespoons of your chosen ingredient (see above). Mix thoroughly with a fork, season with black pepper to taste, and serve. Yum.

POTATOES

[ANNUAL]

| Seed potatoes | March–April ('chit' January–February) | Full sun/ part shade | 30cm apart | June–October |

It's difficult to know what the most exciting part is; digging deep into the earth with your hands, mud up to your elbows, excavating each one with a whimper of joy, or the fact that you have to use 'chitting' potatoes to get them started. Ha ha ha. Chitting potatoes. There's really no greater joy than telling friends you're chitting potatoes on your windowsill.

I naively thought you just bunged seed potatoes into the soil as soon as you bought them, but it turns out you have to put them in a warm place until they sprout. Don't worry; I've learnt a few potato tricks, which we'll get to in just a jiffy.

Come on then. Let's get chitting.

TO PLANT

WHEN: Start preparing early. In late January/early February head to your local garden centre and buy a bag of seed potatoes. I've used Swift Seed First Early with great success, but there are many varieties available. They'll then be ready to plant out around March/April.

WHERE: A sunny, warm windowsill followed by a sunny to medium-sunny spot in your garden.

HOW: Chit potatoes in an egg box, that's my advice. Sit each potato in its own dimple, with the sprouting bits at the top, on a warm sunny windowsill. Then wait. Soon, you'll notice cheeky green shoots. When they reach a good 5cm tall, they're ready to plant.

There's something pleasingly Britain in Blitz about growing your own potatoes. How do you plant them? You build a trench; 10cm deep, nice and straight, in a sunny spot. Line it with a layer of compost, then drop your potatoes in, green shoots upwards. Sprinkle a few slug pellets between the tubers to protect from dastardly underground keel slugs, then cover the whole trench with soil and give them a good water.

SPACE: Plant your tubers at 30cm intervals.

Word on the gardening street is . . . when it comes to container planting, nothing is better than a potato bag. More reliable than big pots, and cheaper. Win win. The big garden centres, DIY chains and online suppliers offer a variety of kits, with bags and seed potatoes included.

Chit as above, then fill an 8-litre potato bag with good-quality multipurpose compost to 2.5cm below the rim. Plunge your tubers into the compost, shoots upwards, 12cm deep and gently cover with compost. Now water and place the bag in a bright, frost-free position.

KEEPING THEM ALIVE

Here's yet another fun potato-growing anomaly. As soon as you see shoots poking out of the earth, cover them over again. Mounding up the earth with your hands to create a sort of man-made molehill is called 'earthing up' in the trade. After a while, the stalk will become strong and full of leaves. As long as you've created that nice big earth mound at the base to begin with, all will be well. 'But why the heck are we doing this? We're not moles', I hear you ponder. Well, the main reason is to prevent new potatoes forming near the surface and turning green (from the sunlight). Green potatoes are poisonous. Preventing death by green potato aside, often more potatoes will form from the buried stems. Huzzah. More potatoes all round.

Feed potato plants every other week with tomato feed – or fancy potato fertiliser – and water when the soil begins to dry out.

HARVESTING

WHEN: Start to harvest earlies as 'new potatoes' as soon as the plants start to flower (about 10 weeks from planting), however the longer you leave them, the bigger they become. Generally speaking, if you wait until two weeks after the stems die/wither and fall over, your potatoes will be just the right big size.

HOW: In fact, you don't harvest potatoes. You 'lift' them. Gently lever a fork back and forth to loosen the soil, then 'sift' for the spuds with your hands. Be sure to have a really thorough rummage in the soil for any strays, otherwise you'll find yourself with surprise potatoes next year. Lifted potatoes are best stored in paper bags or hessian sacks in a dark cool place.

Handy hint: Once you've lifted your potato chums, if it's a nice day, leave them on top of the soil for a few hours to dry and cure their skin before storing.

HOW OFTEN: Harvest your entire potato crop in one go, unless you'd like some earlies.

POTENTIAL DISASTERS

Potato blight. No wonder it caused such an Irish pickle back in the day. It's a *nightmare*. A lot like its tomato cousin, potato blight is evident as a brown watery rot that appears on the leaves and stems. Unlike tomatoes, you can't see if it's reached the potatoes until you dig them up. Reddish-brown patches just below the skin? You've got blight.

Blight spreads very fast. If you're quick, you can remove every single leaf with signs of the disease and hope for the best. If not, the best thing to do is dig them up and save what you can. Luckily, young potatoes are gloriously tasty.

If it looks like it's going to be wet in June, try a protection spray. If blight attacks, dig up and destroy affected plants and plant potatoes somewhere else next year. You can still grow all your other veg in this spot.

Potato blackleg is another bastard of an infection. A black rot at the base of the stem that stunts growth and makes them go yellow. At its worst, it will turn your potatoes grey/brown and rotten. Alas, there's no cure for this little shitter of a disease, so remove and destroy the plants, then make sure you don't grow potatoes in the same place the next year. I've never suffered this, but if you do, get drunk immediately. Cry in a corner. Then try again in 12 months' time. Don't give up.

Potato scab is the last thing to mention, but this one has a cheerier ending. There's no denying it, this disease makes your crop go a bit Mickey Rourke in appearance, but it doesn't matter. Why? Because a quick scrub in the sink, and it comes off. That's right. Completely edible, just as delicious potatoes. Sorted. Any stubborn bits can be nicked out with a knife.

There isn't any control for scab, and you'll know if you have it once you dig your potatoes up (surprise!) but keeping them watered in hot weather will help lessen the likelihood of your crop suffering from it. Use them right away, though, as scabby potatoes don't store well.

FROM THE GARDEN TO THE TABLE

NEW YORK POTATO LATKES

Serves 4

Here's what you'll need:

1kg potatoes, peeled

1 big onion

25g fine matzoh meal or plain flour

1 large free-range egg, beaten

A big sprinkle of sea salt

A few big cracks of black pepper

Olive or vegetable oil, for frying

To serve (optional):

Soured Cream

Apple sauce

or

Good-quality smoked salmon

Homemade horseradish sauce

Fresh chives

If you're making potato latkes for breakfast, you're going to have a bloody brilliant day. There is no bigger breakfast treat. This is also the messiest recipe I've ever had the pleasure to get all over myself and the kitchen of a morning. It relies on activating your potatoes' starch, and good lord do they get sticky. Brace yourselves. I first discovered the joy of potato latkes sitting at a counter in a proper New York deli. They made them right there in front of me, on the hot plate. It was love. Or 'lwuv' if you want to pronounce it in true New York accent.

First of all, it's grating time. Find yourself a large mixing bowl, a sturdy grater and an almost inhuman reserve of energy. Grate all the potatoes and onion on the largest grater setting and mix together in the bowl (I use my hands).

Turn out the grated potato and onion onto a large clean tea towel. Roll it up and squeeze with all your strength to remove as much moisture as you can. The drier the mixture, the better the latkes will turn out.

Drop everything back into the bowl and add the matzoh meal, egg, salt and pepper. Mix well with your hands. If it's getting stuck all over you, it's going well.

In a deep frying pan, heat the oil until moderately hot. Place heaped tablespoons of the mixture into the pan a little distance apart, pushing down on each one with the back of a wooden spoon to flatten them out. Turn down the heat to medium and cook for about 5 minutes on each side, flipping when the edges turn from golden to dark brown. If they brown too quickly, knock the heat back or take the pan off the heat for a minute.

Remove the latkes from the pan and set on kitchen paper to drain. Continue cooking until you've used up all the mixture, then serve while they're still piping hot.

Serve with a dollop each of soured cream and apple sauce, or – my personal favourite – a helping of really good-quality smoked salmon, homemade horseradish sauce (see page 83) and a sprinkle of fresh chives (see page 60).

BEANS: BROAD & RUNNER

[ANNUAL]

| Seedlings | April–July | Full sun/ part shade | 25cm apart | June– September |

I never feel more Mr McGregor than I do with a big crop of flowering runner beans in the veg patch. You'd think it would be lettuce, but no, there's something ludicrously British about picking beans on a sunny day. Imagine Sunday lunch at your grandparents with Bernard Cribbins along for the ride. I know. Best Sunday ever. That said, the recipes on pages 99–101 offer a far more contemporary, inspiring option than the over-cooked nightmare of childhood memories (sorry, Grandma).

Handy hint: Added beany bonus – not only do runner and broad bean flowers attract and nourish bees (see page 242), they're edible for us humans too. There isn't much prettier on a plate than tiny bright orange bean flowers.

TO PLANT

WHEN: Plants will start arriving in garden centres from April onwards. Grab the trowel. We've got some planting to do.

WHERE: In a well-drained sunny or semi-shaded spot in your garden.

HOW: Dig in some compost or well-rotted manure, tuck the little fellas up and water well, scattering a few slug pellets for luck. Now roll up your sleeves for some hard graft. Just like tomatoes, beans need support. But just to confuse, well, me . . . broad beans need different support to runner beans.

Broad bean supports

Get the bamboo stakes out – one for each seedling driven securely into the soil with strings tied in horizontal rows, pulled taught. As they get taller, keep adding strings, as illustrated here. What could be nicer than a wall of beans?

Runner bean supports

Runner beans are a bit more avant garde. But nobody panic. I used to help my dad do this when I was little – it's hard-wired into my noggin. Each bean needs its own pole to wrap around. It's basically a long wigwam – as shown in this handy diagram. Loosely tie the beans to their supports as they grow. You might need to lightly tie each plant to the base of each cane at the beginning, just to set them on their way.

SPACE: Plant your seedlings 25cm apart. If you're going bean crazy and have a lot of seedlings, try a zigzag pattern so they can support each other as they grow. Personally, I have a stupidly small growing space, so I only ever have three or four of each.

Grab the largest container you can find, at least 50cm deep, as wide as possible, fill with potting compost and plant your seedlings in a circle around the outside. Make sure they're at least 20cm apart from each other.

With a bamboo pole pushed into the soil behind each one, create a sort of tepee shape with all the poles meeting at the top. For runner beans, loosely tie each bean to its own pole and repeat as they grow. For broad beans, tie string between the poles in horizontal rows up the canes. Fertilise once a month with a diluted liquid vegetable fertiliser. Tomato feed works for everything.

KEEPING THEM ALIVE

Runner beans like water. Especially when they start to flower. Ensuring that their soil is constantly moist and doesn't dry out is the main way to keep them happy. A good mist of water to their leaves (using the mist setting on your hose or one of those fancy house plant watering spray bottles) will cheer them right up on a hot day and encourage more prolific bean growth. Broad beans also like water, but are most concerned with a good soaking at the start of flowering, then again two weeks later.

For both runner and broad beans pinch out the 'growing set' (the little bunch of growing leaves/stuff at the top of the stem) when they reach the top of their supports. This will make them put all their beany energy into growing beans.

To encourage all the seed pods to form, and to reduce blackfly problems on your broad beans, pinch out all the tips of the beans once the lowest level of flowers have begun to form seed pods (baby broad beans . . . yes). The best bit? You get to eat these delicious little bean shoots in your salad. They're unexpectedly tasty.

HARVESTING

WHEN: For runner beans, pick when 15–20cm long. For broad beans, once you can see the beans begin to swell inside their pods (you can quite easily see the shape beneath the surface), they're ready to go.

HOW: For both runner and broad beans, simply hold the bean in one hand while gently snapping it off its branch with the other, right at the base of the bean. Easy.

HOW OFTEN: Runner beans first. Now, what I'm about to tell you is very important. It's vital, essential and indeed paramount, that you keep picking your runner beans – on a daily basis if necessary. Even if your freezer is full and your friends and family are crying out for you to stop. Why? Because if your pods start reaching maturity (getting too big) . . . your plants will stop flowering, and that means NO MORE BEANS. I know. Harrowing. Check in every day or so, and you'll be able to get up to another 8 weeks of bean production out of them.

Broad beans are less needy, though they have their own weird preference for the order you pick them . . . Harvest in stages, starting with the lowest pod first. Small beans are sweeter and more tender, so don't worry if you can't hold yourself back.

If you find yourself suffering from acute broad bean impatience, small immature pods can be cooked and eaten whole. Try them sizzling on a hot plate with a glug of olive oil, a generous crack of sea salt and some chopped fresh chilli.

POTENTIAL DISASTERS

Beans are pretty mellow. They don't have anything scary like blight to contend with and, luckily, the most common bean problems are easy dealt with if caught early. So keep your eyes peeled, bean watchers.

Slugs and snails, my dastardly slimy garden adversaries; these are RIGHT little tossers when your seedlings are young. It happens early in the morning. You potter out to have a look at your carefully planted little friends before work, when you see it . . . carnage. Leaves munched to within an inch of their lives. Tattered stalks lying sideways in despair. The answer? Copper tape around the edges of your bed, beer traps, sawdust – for me, nothing has worked except the bright blue pellets of doom. Scatter them early, on the day you plant them, then you can sleep easy.

Blackfly and aphids are also overly fond of beans, the little rogues. They suck sap, excrete sticky honeydew and promote the growth of black sooty moulds. Disaster all round. But not if you have a bottle of Timmy's Homemade Fly Destroying Spray of Awesomeness to hand (see page 30). Use your finger and thumb to squash any flies you find on the leaves, then go crazy with the spray. Again, catch this early and your plants will carry on as though nothing happened.

No, or not many, beans, is the worst problem you'll come across because – brace yourself – there's nothing you can do until next year. It's more likely in runner beans, but it's heartbreaking when it happens. It's usually due to lack of moisture and/or lack of pollination by insects. The best defence is to make sure you've dug in plenty of well-rotted manure and compost into the soil before planting, as this will help with moisture- and nutrient-retention deep down around the roots. A sheltered area will encourage bees to visit and pollinate your plants, as will bee-attracting plants throughout your garden. Skip to pages 238–242 for a full 'Save De Bees' guide to planting. Sorry, bean lovers. Let's look at some recipes to cheer ourselves up.

FROM THE GARDEN TO THE TABLE

RUNNER BEAN KIMCHI

Makes 1 litre

Here's what you'll need:

750g runner beans, top and tailed, halved and shredded lengthways

6 spring onions, finely chopped

1 daikon radish, grated (try Oriental stores, healthfood stores or the Internet; or substitute with 10 white radishes)

10 red radishes, grated

5 garlic cloves, crushed

1½ tbsp unrefined sugar

1 thumb-sized piece of ginger, peeled and finely grated

2 tbsp sea salt

3 tbsp red chilli flakes (I crumble whole dried ones, seeds removed)

1 sterilised (see overleaf) 1-litre screw-top jar

Yes, kimchi is trendier than a converted street food truck full of rainbow-haired blogger/models selling cronuts, but you know the thing about some trends? Every now and then, they introduce you to something truly delicious. For me, kimchi is one of these happy occasions. It's outrageously tasty, hitting all the umami buttons. In fact, it's my new favourite condiment, going with everything from an open sandwich to grilled chicken, hot from the BBQ.

Health benefits aside, making kimchi has a suitably 'mad scientist' appeal, taking us into the brave new world of fermenting. In this recipe, I've thrown caution to the wind and replaced the more traditional cabbage with runner beans. They look lovely, have a beautiful texture (maintaining a satisfying bite) and add an unmistakably bright and runner-beany flavour to the mix. N.B. This will take 5–8 days to do its magical kimchi thing. Patience, young grasshopper.

Tip all your ingredients into the largest bowl you have, adding the salt and chilli flakes last.

Handy hint 1: The most time-consuming part of kimchi is the chopping, shredding and grating involved. For the beans, I'd highly recommend eitther a food processor with a shredding attachment/setting or one of those lovely old-fashioned runner bean shredders you find in kitchen shops.

Now it's time to massage your runner bean mix. Thoroughly wash your hands, roll up your sleeves and get in there, squeezing and massaging your veg for about 10 minutes. Set aside and let everything rest, including yourself. The salt will encourage your vegetables to 'sweat' out some of their water. After 10 minutes, repeat for another 10 minutes, by which time your beans should have softened, releasing a little more water.

Transfer to your 1-litre Mason jar, pressing down firmly to release any last air bubbles and so that there is some liquid at the top of the jar. Add 2 tablespoons of the leftover kimchi liquid and then secure the lid loosely, to allow air to escape during fermentation.

Then it's the waiting game. Sit your jar somewhere warmish (room temperature, or next to a fridge) and keep an eye on it for 2–4 days until bubbles start to appear. Then pop the jar in the fridge. Around 3–4 days later, it's ready to eat as a fresh, mellow kimchi. However, kimchi's flavour develops over time, getting stronger and more sour. Test every few days. I like it at the two week stage, but I rarely wait that long for the first few spoonfuls.

Unopened runner bean kimchi will keep happily for 2–3 months if sealed. Once opened, keep in the fridge, always use a clean fork or spoon to dish out and try to finish within two months.

Handy hint 2: Leftover kimchi liquid makes a brilliant marinade. Cover a few chicken breasts with it and leave overnight and you'll be halfway to an excellent stir-fried noodle lunch.

HOW TO STERILISE JARS

I hoard empty jars, much to Tim's dismay – all shapes and sizes. You can buy them, of course, but this is far cheaper and they look cool all mixed up.

Sterilising jars is easy. Heat your oven to 140°C/275°F/gas 1. Wash the jars in hot, soapy water, then rinse well. Place them on a baking sheet and put them in the oven to dry completely. If you're using fancy Kilner jars, boil the rubber seals, as dry heat damages them. Use oven gloves – they get bloody hot, as a scar on my finger can attest.

COAL-CHARRED BROAD BEANS IN THEIR PODS

Serves 4 as a
tapas-style starter

If ever there was a vegetable dish made for the BBQ, this is it. It's a sort of 'padron peppers' for the bean world: smoky, fresh, simple and fun. Sitting in the garden with friends, popping hot beans out of their charred shells, sipping on an ice-cold Chablis? Life doesn't get much happier than this.

Here's what you'll need:

A big bowl of broad beans, in their pods

A few big glugs of extra virgin olive oil, plus extra for serving

A good crumble of sea salt, plus extra for serving

A generous few cracks of black pepper

The juice of ½ lemon

First of all, get your BBQ going. Make sure you have a nice pile of coals built up in the middle.

Meanwhile, on to the seriously minimal prep. Wash your broad beans, blot them dry, then toss in a big bowl with the olive oil, salt and pepper. Prep done.

When the BBQ coals are white, spread them out evenly and lower your grill to as close to the coals as possible. Place the beans on the grill and cook for 5–6 minutes, until beautifully charred, turning halfway through.

To serve, arrange them on a giant platter for the middle of the table, drizzle with lemon juice, a splash more olive oil and a good sprinkle of sea salt. Heaven.

VERY IMPORTANT POINT: Don't be the fool who eats the stringy pods. This is a messy, 'pop them out of their charred shells' sort of snack. I opt for the 'giant edamame beans' approach, sucking/dragging them out with my teeth so as to make the most of all that oily smoky salty taste. Classy.

COURGETTES

[ANNUAL]

Seedlings   April–July   Full sun/   1m apart   July–October
part shade

Good news . . . courgettes are, beyond a shadow of a doubt, the easiest vegetable to grow. One tiny seedling and you'll have a steady crop of fresh, tasty courgettes for weeks and weeks in the summer.

I've been growing 'Taxi' or 'Soleil' courgettes for the last few years – bright yellow, smooth-skinned little fellas, which look lovely in salads, have a bright fresh taste and are so tender you can eat them raw or lightly pickled, Swedish-style (see page 107). These are early maturing and high yielding, which basically means that for impatient gardeners (me) you'll get courgettes sooner – then keep on getting them. However, the following advice applies to all courgette varieties.

TO PLANT

WHEN: In late April/early May you'll see courgette seedlings start to arrive in garden centres.

WHERE: Find the sunniest spot in your garden. Courgettes love the sunshine. They're like Joey Essex.

HOW: Dig a small-football-sized hole in your bed and chuck in some well-rotted manure or compost. Pop the little chap in, tuck him up so that the soil's nice and firm but not rock solid around him (you don't want him wobbling about), then give him a good old soak.

SPACE: If you're planting more than one, make sure they're a good metre away from each other. This puppy's going to get BIG. Silly big. Ours reached the width of a swarthy man's shoulders last year. He's got large leaves and likes to stretch. Try not to cramp his style.

If you're planting in a pot, use the biggest one you can get your hands on. At least 30–35cm wide, as deep as you can find. Then follow the instructions above.

KEEPING THEM ALIVE

Courgettes are thirsty little critters. Keep them well watered and you're basically good to go. On a hot day I quickly chuck some water at them before work, then water them again when I get back.

Apart from that, it's a good idea to give them a feed every now and then. Every few weeks, sprinkle tomato feed at the base of the stem to keep Mr Courgette happy. A sprinkle of fertiliser pellets across the soil at the beginning of the season will keep nutrients topped up, but it's best to follow the instructions on the packet as each one's a little different.

Good old courgettes. Truly, a low-maintenance gardener's dream.

HARVESTING

WHEN: Courgettes are crazy productive. At the height of the growing season you'll have anywhere between 10 and 20 courgettes on your plant at any one time.

As a guide, harvest when the courgettes reach around 10cm long. They're at their very best eaten that day but will keep quite happily for a few days in the fridge.

HOW: To harvest, go and get a sharp knife from the kitchen then carefully slice them at the base; the green knobbly bit where it joins the main trunk of the plant. BE CAREFUL. Sure, you're brandishing a sharp knife, don't go maiming yourself. But mainly . . . be careful of the courgette. Tim is a notorious accidental destroyer of courgette plants. Truly a scourge of the Cucurbita Family. Knives are sharp, and unless my biology GCSE has failed me, plants need leaves.

HOW OFTEN: Try to harvest a few times a week. The more you take, the more your lunatic plant will grow.

POTENTIAL DISASTERS

Well there's the whole Accidentally-Slicing-Leaves-Off thing, but there are a few other things to keep an eye on, too.

Flower head rot. I only realised this existed when it happened to me. Luckily, there's an easy solution; as soon as those beautiful big courgette flowers start growing . . . pick 'em – at the giant opening-out stage. Keep an eye on them as you water. Is the top of the courgette ok, just where it meets the flower? To be honest, I always lose one or two to flower head rot – usually in busy weeks when I haven't been paying attention. Don't cry. It doesn't spread to the plant and if you catch it early, you can simply chop the squishy bit off and eat the rest of the courgette. Phew.

As for all those lovely flowers? Fire up the frying pan – it's time for the sheer Italian joy of Fried courgette flowers. (Recipe overleaf).

Powdery mildew. I've found this on leaves a few times, usually late in the summer, when the courgette plant is throwing out vegetables left, right and centre. It doesn't seem to be a big deal, but does suggest a lack of water. The best thing to do is add a layer of compost/well-rotted manure/mulch to the base of the plant. This will help to reduce evaporation from the soil.

FROM THE GARDEN TO THE TABLE

SWEDISH FRESH PICKLED COURGETTE

Serves 4 as a side

Here's what you'll need

1 banana shallot, diced

1 small bunch of dill, roughly chopped

3 yellow courgettes

2 tiny cucumbers (similar in size to your courgettes)

100ml cider vinegar

65g white sugar

50ml water

Flowers from your courgette plants and nasturtium plants (see page 214 – optional)

Having spent a year commuting to Sweden every week with work, I became accidentally hooked on pickles, pickling and all things pickled. Sweet, sharp and fresh, this recipe is summer on a garden table. Especially when served on the side of fresh tuna tartare and tiny toasts. There's a bit of cucumber in here, too, to balance out the flavours, but your bright yellow courgettes are the real stars of the culinary show.

Pop the shallot and dill into a medium-sized bowl. Take a potato peeler and run it along your courgettes and cucumbers to create long, fine ribbons of flesh – leave the skins on to add colour to the dish. This is weirdly satisfying. Add to the shallots and dill and put to one side.

Pour the vinegar, sugar and water into a small pan, then bring to the boil. As soon as it starts bubbling, turn off the heat, pour over your courgette mixture and give it all a good stir.

Cover with cling film and leave in the fridge for at least 1½ hours (though it's at its best after 3) before serving. I like to arrange it ribbon by ribbon, folding them onto the plate in an arty manner. To finish, slice the courgette and nasturtium flowers roughly and scatter over the top to look like a badass Michelin chef. 'Oh this? Just a few things from the garden.'

FRIED COURGETTE FLOWERS TUSCAN-STYLE

Serves 4 as an antipasti-style starter

Here's what you'll need:

About 16 closed courgette flowers

120g of white flour

200ml of ice-cold sparkling water (with the rest of the bottle on standby)

A big pinch of salt

A few cracks of black pepper

Olive oil, for frying

Squeeze of lemon juice, to serve

This is so tasty that I sometimes dream about it in the dead of winter. And so easy that we should probably keep it 'entre nous'. Though that's French. This is the genuine Tuscan way of doing it, with sparkling water for the batter. The bubbles leave tiny spaces in the mixture that fill with air once they hit the oil, making for a lovely light, fluffy batter. Your courgette flowers need to be closed for this recipe, so grab a torch and venture into the garden at night, armed with a sharp knife. What could go wrong? (Or you could just pop out first thing in the morning.)

First up, dry your flowers with a paper towel, remove any bugs and pull out their stamens inside the petals.

Then it's on to the batter. Sift the white flour into a big bowl. Get a fork and slowly start to mix in the chilled sparkling water. The batter should be as thin as possible – the consistency of milk – so keep going if 200ml isn't quite enough, beating with the fork to get rid of any big lumps. It's not an exact science, so don't stress yourself out. Have a drink.

Stir in a big pinch of salt and a healthy crack of black pepper then dunk each courgette flower into the batter mix and pop on a plate to one side.

Heat about 8cm of olive oil in a frying pan – keeping an eye on it to make sure it doesn't start smoking. When the oil's really hot, pop the battered courgette flowers in with a pair of tongs, one by one, turning when golden brown.

Once they're done on both sides, whip them out and blot them on a piece of kitchen paper. Serve as fast as you can – they're best just out of the pan – with a squeeze of fresh lemon, a large glass of cold white wine and a bad Italian accent.

PEAS:

MANGETOUT & SUGAR SNAP

[ANNUAL]

| Seedlings | April–May | Full sun/ part shade | 15cm apart | June– September |

Time for a confession. My name's Hollie and I'm a pea addict. Off the wagon. On the (pea) sauce. I suffer from genuine heart palpitations if I don't have at least two bags of petit pois in the freezer at all times*. If peas are involved . . . I'm in. So imagine my excitement when pea season comes around in the garden.

The easiest peas to grow are mangetout and sugar snap. In fact, they work so well that I haven't bothered attempting any other varieties. The fear of losing a crop of precious, precious peas is too great.

*That's blatantly a terrible exaggeration for dramatic effect. But I do get angsty. No one wants pea angst.

TO PLANT

WHEN: Mangetout and sugar snap seedlings start arriving in garden centres from early April.

WHERE: Would it surprise you to know that peas want a sunny spot in the veg patch? For crying out loud, doesn't everyone? Where's a haphazard gardener to put all these plants? The answer, with both mangetout and sugar snaps, is at the back. They get very tall, but not particularly wide, leaving lots of space for diminutive vegetable friends, such as carrots, beetroot, lettuce and the odd radish at the front.

HOW: Water the ground well before digging a little hole for each plant, digging in a little compost or well-rotted manure (a sprinkle should do it), then plant them in a straight line.

Everyone seems to have their own pea-supporting style, but the basic rule is thus: one pole per plant, firmly stuck into the ground for the peas to grow up. I find tightly fixed netting attached to the poles works best, to create a great big wall for them to grow against and hang onto with their little pea tendrils. It also saves you tying 1,000,000 knots for horizontal strings. You might need to lightly tie each plant to the base of each cane at the beginning, just to set them on their way.

SPACE: Plant your peas 15cm apart from each other, in a long row.

Peas are almost identical to beans where pots are concerned. Once again, it's time for the largest container you can find or fit into your space, at least 50cm deep and as wide as possible. Fill with good-quality potting compost then plant your little pea plants in a circle around the outside. Make sure they're at least 8cm apart from each other to give them room to grow, then it's time to construct them a little house.

With a bamboo pole pushed into the soil behind each one, create a sort of tipi shape – all the poles meeting at the top (see diagram, page 95). Tie a series of horizontal string rows up the canes for them to grow up. As above, you'll probably need to lightly tie each plant to the base of each cane at the beginning.

KEEPING THEM ALIVE

Peas are particularly easy to look after, bless 'em. The main thing to keep an eye out for is the first sign of flowering. As soon as you see a blossom appear, get the hose out (or watering can) and give them a twice-daily water, morning and evening. Continue for two weeks and they'll be set right up for an abundant harvest.

Other than that, I like to add a mulch around the base of the plants to keep moisture in as the sun shines. A layer of compost or very well-rotted manure will work splendidly.

HARVESTING

WHEN: When the pods reach about 7cm long.

HOW: Start at the bottom of your pea plants, working your way up. I carefully snap each pod off with a quick turn and pull of the wrist, but if you're of a clumsy or nervous disposition, grab a pair of scissors. Ta da. Let the pea fest commence.

HOW OFTEN: Get picking, pea fans. The more you pick, the more your plants will grow. In fact, if you stop picking, or leave the pods to get too big, the plant will stop producing flowers and peas altogether. Crazy old Nature.

POTENTIAL DISASTERS

My pea mania makes me particularly paranoid about pea problems. That's a lot of 'p's. Luckily, as we're growing from garden-centre seedlings, the mangetout and sugar snaps of the UK tend to be disease-resistant varieties. That just leaves 'critters' to deal with.

Slugs and snails are just as keen on peas as they are on beans. Their stealth attacks are relentless. It's my Vietnam. Get the slug pellets down early and hope for the best. Your plants can take a minor munching, but I did once have to replace three plants – the one time I didn't put down slug pellets . . .

Birds are complete reprobates where peas are concerned. Especially the damn pigeon. ALWAYS the damn pigeon. The problem is . . . we're too alike. A shame that my true Moriarty is a ratty old sky rat, but there we are. They like peas just as much as me. Leaves and all. My dearly departed, embarrassingly right-wing, all-round-dangerous eccentric of a grandfather solved the problem by lying in wait with a .22 rifle, shooting them dead. He did the same with squirrels, hanging their tails from the apple tree as a warning to their squirrel friends. Then again, my granddad was stark raving mad. Lest I turn you all into serial killers, how about we all agree on this . . . netting. Purchased from any garden centre or DIY shop, draped over your peas, and secured with twigs at the bottom. End the violence people. Make peas, not war.

Handy hint: The greatest mangetout and sugar snap recipe – just eat them. Honestly, if they make it out of the garden and into the kitchen I'll be impressed. At most, a couple of minutes steamed or boiled to soften them a little and release their sweetness. Maybe go nuts with a sprinkle of sea salt and a crack of black pepper. Other than that, I'd be an idiot to interrupt their perfection with a faffy recipe.

Hooray for peas.

TOMATOES

[PERENNIAL]

| Seedlings | April–June | Full sun/ part shade | 60cm apart | July–October |

Good old tomatoes. Strictly speaking, a fruit, but I've put them in the vegetable section nonetheless. Basic biology aside, I simply don't believe in savoury fruit.

Tomatoes are easy peasy but what *isn't* easy is choosing which variety to grow. There are so many, it's mind-curdling. My basic rule when choosing is . . . what do I want to eat?

Mini Italian plums are super easy to grow, sweet and tasty and make squillions to harvest. Equally, 'Sweet Million' are total show-offs – an intensely flavoured small red tomato. Or try 'Sungold' – a bite-sized variety, bright orange when it ripens, voted 'the sweetest tomato ever'.

I haven't bought a single summer supermarket tomato since I started growing them myself. In fact they're so prolific that I spend my days giving them to friends, family and passing strangers.

TO PLANT

WHEN: In late April/early May you'll see tomato seedlings start to arrive in garden centres.

WHERE: Build their new home in a sunny part of your garden.

HOW: Before planting, you're going to have to do a bit of construction work. Grab a beer. Then take a look on Google. There are all sorts of ways to tie your tomato supports, but I opt for the 'long wigwam' style, pictured. A double line of stakes lined up, tied at the top opposite each other with a long pole keeping them together. Then I tie a series of horizontal supports, in long lines, at intervals up the structure.

Bloody hell. It's like the Scouts.

Then it's simple. Grab your trowel, dig a little hole at the base of each pole, plant the seedlings, then thoroughly soak them and sing them a little good luck song.

SPACE: Make sure your seedlings are a good 60cm apart, with their own poles. If they're looking a bit louche, tie them loosely with garden twine.

In late April/early May you'll find specialist trailing varieties coming into big garden centres (many even sell seedlings pre-planted in colourful hanging pots). I'm particularly taken with a variety called 'Tomato Hundreds and Thousands.' Their name doesn't lie. The more you pick these tiny toms, the more they grow. If you only have a tiny space, this is your summer tomato crop SORTED. I eat them like sweets as I potter around the garden.

You might also try ye olde hanging basket. Tomatoes do freakishly well in these.

If you're planting in a pot, the bigger the better. At least 30cm, but 60cm is better. Just remember . . . one plant per pot. They're big bastards and argue, *Game Of Thrones* style, if they have to share room. Put a few stones in the bottom for drainage, then fill with a good-quality potting compost and plant as above.

KEEPING THEM ALIVE

Tomatoes need a good watering every day, unless it rains. They also like a slosh of tomato feed every two weeks from their first flower appearing. Easies.

Now . . . a word on pruning. *Serious horticultural voice. And eyebrow.* Before we go any further, I should tell you . . . my tomatoes have been known to get so out of control, NATO was once put on alert. Every year, I start with such good intentions. Then comes 'Tomatogeddon'. Horticultural humiliation. But together, we shall learn how to grow respectable, prolific tomato plants.

Pruning or pinching away new leaf growth will encourage your plant to concentrate all his growing powers into the tomatoes, rather than leaves. Who wants leaves? We're after tomatoes here, people. When your plant reaches roughly 45cm tall, wait for his first flowers to blossom, then remove all the leaves and growing tips below that point.

Now you have a decision to make: do you want one main growing stem, or more? Single-stem tomatoes don't need a lot of space, so are a good option for containers and small spaces, but they produce fewer tomatoes than multi-stemmed plants. In a raised bed, I aim for a three- or four-stemmer.

To grow a two-stemmed plant, let a growth tip or shoot grow from the leaf axil or 'V' above the first blossom cluster. This will become the second stem. To grow a three-stemmed plant, let the growth tip grow from the leaf axil directly above the second stem. And so on.

Check your plant once a week, pinching out unwanted growing tips. When your tomatoes reach the same height as their supports, pinch out all the new growing tips.

Yes, it falls into the 'minor ball ache' league, but it's worth it; after a few weeks your plant will get the picture and concentrate on nothing but sweet, sweet tomato growing.

Handy hint: Don't pinch away a growth tip too soon. You need at least two sets of leaves to grow on a side shoot before pinching it off. Press your thumb and a finger together, hold on just above the two sets of leaves, and pull it off quickly. This will protect the stem from sun damage.

HARVESTING

Run. Get the biggest bowl you own. Get a backup bowl. Get a wheelbarrow. For lo . . . the tomatoes are upon us.

WHEN: Once they turn from green to red, yellow or orange, depending on variety.

HOW: Whenever you come across a firm, ripe, evenly coloured tomato – PULL. Fruit by fruit, with a quick yank and a slight twist.

HOW OFTEN: At the height of the season you'll find yourself picking tomatoes every day. Then towards the end of the season you'll find yourself with a problem . . . lots of green tomatoes. Fear not, there are many ways to use these miscreant teenagers. You can hang them, still on the branch, in a cool garden shed (or cupboard) to ripen, line them up on a warm sunny windowsill, snuggle them in with a banana, or cook with them (see pages 122–125).

POTENTIAL DISASTERS

One of the most common problems you'll notice is **leaf curling**. Very often this is due to an aphid attack. Planting nasturtiums and garlic near your tomatoes will repel these sneaky aphids with their smell (see companion planting p29), or whip up a batch of Timmy's magic pest-killing formula (recipe page 30).

Lumps and 'nodules' on leaves indicate that the roots are too wet . . . so stop watering them so much.

Then there are these odd, dry, brown, dead patches that appear late in the season. What on earth are these . . . ? **Blight.** I didn't even realise I'd been hit by blight for the first two years. After weeks of solid tomato production, I assumed the plants had reached the end of their natural tomatoey life.

Spotting it early is key. Is it late summer? Can you see brown lesions or watery rot on the stems and leaves? Shrivelling? In wet weather, is there a fine white fungus around these areas and under the leaves? Yes? Congratulations. You've got blight. Let Operation-Stop-It-Spreading commence. Remove infected leaves immediately and put them in a garden waste bag. When infection reaches 25 per cent of a stem, cut it off right at the base.

Blight is far more likely in wet weather, so from June onwards, use a protective spray when rain is forecast. However, in a wet summer it will only slow the fungus.

Every three years, if you're growing your tomatoes in a bed, switch them to somewhere else. This will help prevent a build-up of the blight fungus in your soil. Damn blight. It truly is the herpes of the tomato world.

FROM THE GARDEN TO THE TABLE

HOMEMADE TOMATO KETCHUP

Makes roughly 2½ litres

Here's what you'll need:

Around 3.5kg tomatoes, roughly chopped

1 onion, roughly diced

1 head of garlic, peeled and roughly chopped

90g salt

900g golden sugar

600ml red wine vinegar

½ tsp cayenne pepper or dried chilli flakes

1 tsp whole cloves

1 fennel bulb, trimmed and finely chopped

2 thumb-sized pieces of ginger, peeled and finely chopped

Did someone say 'tomato glut'? Fear not. This is the modern alternative to chutney. Bacon sandwiches will never be the same again.

Be warned; this ketchup recipe is tasty. DEAD tasty. As you make it, you'll be all, 'cool, I can give this as presents to my deeply impressed friends'. Once you've tried it, you'll quickly change to, 'get off. It's mine.'

One thing . . . the colour of your ketchup will depend on the colour of your tomatoes. Red tomatoes: red ketchup. Yellow tomatoes: yellow ketchup. Unripe green tomatoes: green ketchup with a tang to the tastebuds. A mixture of everything: brown ketchup. This is what I generally end up with, and, as well as being a hilarious breakfast prank when guests mistake it for HP sauce, it's delicious. Use whatever's in your garden. It will taste wonderful.

First of all, rummage about in your cupboards, and pull out the biggest heavy bottomed pan you own, or divide the ingredients between two smaller pans.

Then it's very simple. Bundle all the ingredients into the pan and simmer . . . for about 3 hours. Give it a taste. You can wiggle the flavours around by adding a little more sugar and so on – especially if you're using green tomatoes.

Don't get over-excited and run off to the cinema while your ketchup bubbles away. It's a little needy. Stir it regularly so it doesn't catch and burn on the bottom.

Lift the ketchup off the heat and leave to cool slightly before pouring the whole lot into a food processor (in batches), or use a hand blender to blend to a lovely thick 'ketchuppy' consistency.

Using a sterilised funnel, pour into sterilised bottles and jars (see page 100). And there we have it: homemade tomato ketchup. Store in a cool dark cupboard. Once opened, it should be stored in the fridge, where it will keep happily for up to a month.

NEW ORLEANS FRIED GREEN TOMATOES

Serves 4 as a
laid-back starter

I first tried these, as the name suggests, in New Orleans, in a scruffy little restaurant on Magazine Street. They also served $2 martinis, so it's all a bit of an alcohol-induced blur to be honest, but after trying many different recipes, this is the closest I've got to that delicious first bite.

Obviously, this recipe requires green tomatoes. The bigger the better. I make this towards the end of the season, when they've given up turning red, but feel free to pick a few big unripe toms at any point. Your plant will grow more.

Here's what you'll need:

1 large egg,
lightly beaten

110ml buttermilk*

60g self-raising
cornmeal mix**

A big crunch
of sea salt

A big pinch of
black pepper

60g plain
white flour

3 big green
tomatoes cut
into discs

Vegetable oil,
for frying

In a big bowl, whisk together the egg and buttermilk until evenly mixed. In a shallow dish, combine your cornmeal mix, salt, pepper and 30g of flour. In another bowl, spread out the remaining flour.

Dunk the tomato slices first in the flour, then into the egg, then into the cornmeal, giving them a good coating on both sides. This is a wonderfully messy production line. Batter all over the place.

Meanwhile, pour the oil to a depth of about 2½cm in a large heavy-bottomed frying pan and heat until piping hot. Drop the battered tomatoes, in batches, into the hot oil and cook for about 2 minutes on each side, until golden. Use tongs to remove them, drain on kitchen paper and sprinkle with salt. Serve with a drizzle of hot sauce and sprinkle of paprika. Oh . . . and a vodka martini.

*If you don't have buttermilk, you can make your own. For 110ml of buttermilk, add ½ tablespoon of lemon juice or vinegar to 110ml of milk and stir.

**Self-raising cornmeal mix is hard to get hold of, but easy to make. Take 60g plain cornmeal, add 1½ teaspoons baking powder, ½ teaspoon salt and stir until mixed thoroughly.

BEETROOT

[ANNUAL]

| Seedlings | May–July | Full sun/ part shade | 10cm apart | July– November |

Ah, Mr Beetroot, you reliable old rogue.

If I can give you nothing else in life, let me bestow you with this . . . the gift of growing your own beetroot. The worst gardener in the world (my sister) will find it hard to destroy a beetroot. No matter what size, shape or malformed little monster you manage to create, it will taste amazing. Deep, sweet, earthy and fresh all at the same time.

Weirdly, considering how many heirloom varieties you find on fancy restaurant plates, there's basically 'beetroot' on offer – a bolt-resistant strain, in the traditional red/purple hue that beetroot's famous for. Though there are all sorts of varieties in seed form, it's tricky to track down more interesting seedlings, although you might be able to find a rainbow mix of seedlings online.

TO PLANT

WHEN: In early May you'll start seeing beetroot seedlings arrive on the shelves.

WHERE: Some plants are divas. They demand full, uninterrupted sunshine or wither and die in an act of hysterical defiance. Others will get by with a little less. I'd put Mr Beetroot in the 'get by with a little less' category. My garden's small and narrow, the further down the raised bed you go, the fewer hours of sunshine it gets in a day. For the last few years, I've put my beetroot halfway along. They get a decent-ish amount of sun, and haven't complained a bit.

So, if you're running out of sunny spots, opt for a medium-to-low-sun spot for your beetroot. They'll be fine and dandy.

HOW: Before planting, rake a layer of well-rotted compost into the planting area and sprinkle a few fertiliser pellets. Dig a little hole and pop in your beetroot seedlings, then tuck them in with soil and water well. As with carrots make sure you plant each tiny plant seperately, rather than the clumps they sometimes come planted in.

SPACE: Beetroot grow up rather than out, needing only 10cm between each plant. They don't grow particularly high either, so plant in front of a taller crop, such as peas.

As ever, the bigger the pot the better. Less than 30cm diameter and your beetroot will start getting angry. But your pot doesn't need to be particularly deep – just a decent size with stones or broken bits of pots in the bottom for drainage, filled with a good-quality potting compost and planted as above. Beetroot ready to go.

KEEPING THEM ALIVE

While beetroot are pretty laid back, like Gizmo, they don't enjoy being over-watered. If they get too drenched they'll rebel, growing more leaf and less beetroot. On the whole, normal rainfall will be enough to keep them happy. In dry spells, water every 10–14 days. If you're doing an insouciant 'water the whole garden from the door' move, try to avoid the area with the beetroot. Remember what happened in Gremlins.

HARVESTING

WHEN: Beetroot are so transparent, man. Their tops grow above soil, so it's easy to tell how big they are. Roughly speaking, pick them when they're between a golf ball and a tennis ball size. Small beetroot are sweet and fresh, bigger beetroot have that earthy, deep taste, but much bigger than a tennis ball and they won't taste as good.

HOW: With one hand, take hold of your beetroot's leaves, just above his head. With the other, use a small fork to scoop under the roots and lever it out. Lo . . . a beetroot is born.

HOW OFTEN: I harvest mine alternately. A round of small golf-ball beetroot first, leaving space for the rest of them to reach tennis-ball size weeks later. I know, pretty impressive tactics. I'd love to take credit for such guile, but it was Timmy's gardening genius of a granddad who taught me this trick.

POTENTIAL DISASTERS

One of the only risks to your beetroot is **'bolting'**. Simply speaking, this is when plants get over-excited, shoot up, and start flowering. Why is this a problem? If your beetroot's making flowers, he's not making nice fat edible roots. Most seedling varieties are bolt resistant, but a sudden cold spell or prolonged drought could set it off. Unfortunately, there's not a lot you can do once it's bolted. If caught early, you can try twisting and snapping off the bolting stem (never cut it). Quite often, this saves the day. Phew.

The only other major fudge up I've fallen victim to . . . is the damned **pigeon**. At the young, just planted stage, all veg are at their most vulnerable. Slug pellets are essential, and you can put a net over plants but nothing can protect them from a clumsy pigeon.

FROM THE GARDEN TO THE TABLE

SALT-BAKED BEETROOT

Serves 2 as a side dish, or 4 as a starter with smoked salmon

Here's what you'll need:

1 nice round beetroot

1 boxes of Maldon Sea Salt (or any good-quality salt)

2–3 sprigs of thyme

As my splendid friend, Ben 'Yes Chef' Christopherson said when I ran him through this recipe, 'I love this, it tastes amazing, and there is the element of "why the hell am I doing this, this can't possibly be right?", which all the best recipes should have.' Wise words, Ben. Wise words.

Preheat your oven to 160C°/300°F/gas 2.

Rummage around for the smallest ovenproof dish that will fit your beetroot as snuggly as possible. Pour a generous layer of salt into the dish, making a large dimple to rest your beetroot on, and pop him in. Add the thyme on top and around your beetroot, then keep pouring salt until your beetroot is entombed in a salt mountain. Then pop him in the oven for 45–60 minutes.

The beetroot is done when a sharp knife slips in easily. A bit like pasta, the perfect texture of beetroot is down to personal taste. I like it a little firm in the middle, so take it out after 50 minutes. It also depends on the size of your beetroot, so pop him back in for a bit longer if he isn't quite done.

Once cooked, remove the dish from the oven and leave to cool for a few minutes. Then dive on in there and rescue your baked beetroot. (I let the salt cool, then keep it in a Kilner jar to use again.) Slice his skin and ends off by running a knife from top to bottom, gently peeling it away. Carefully slice into thin slices, then arrange in an impressive, arty fashion on a plate.

An excellent side dish, or delicious starter served with slithers of smoked salmon, watercress, good olive oil and freshly grated horseradish.

SAUTÉED BEETROOT LEAVES WITH GARLIC AND CHILLI

Serves 2 as
a side

This is a simple recipe, but a revelation. You can eat beetroot leaves too! What a plant. A bit similar to spinach, but more colourful and lighter in taste. I make this as a tasty vegetable side for all sorts of meals. It's particularly good with steak.

Here's what you'll need:

A big glug of
olive oil

A couple of
garlic cloves,
sliced thinly

1 or 2 dried red
chillies (to taste),
seeds removed,
crumbled

A big handful of
beetroot leaves,
roughly chopped,
and stalks,
separated and
finely chopped

A crunch of
sea salt

A crack of
black pepper

In a non-stick or heavy bottomed frying pan, heat the oil, then pop in the garlic and chilli. Sizzle until golden, then add the chopped beetroot stalks for 1–2 minutes, until tender. Finally, add in the beetroot leaves and wilt. This is best done by eye, but should take a minute or so.

Add a crunch of sea salt, a crack of black pepper and serve immediately. Mmmmm . . . I can almost smell it now.

Handy hint: Beetroot bulbs keep fresher for longer if you cut their stalks off straight away. Pop them in the fridge and they'll be happy for a good few days. Beetroot stalks and leaves, on the other hand, stay fresh and sprightly if you pop them into a glass of water.

OVERWINTERING

ERIN GWEG

OVERWINTERING
VEGETABLES

Pull on a bobble hat and sturdy yourself with a swig of Lagavulin Single Malt, we're going outside. In winter.

Yes, the wonder of growing vegetables over the Yuletide months is upon us. You won't be harvesting them until spring, but their cheery green foliage will go a long way to brightening up the barren emptiness of a forlorn winter garden.

Growing overwintering veg also means that, even as you shelter on the sofa watching your third Netflix boxset in a row, you're actually being very productive. 'Can't you see I'm growing onions? Now stop berating me and pass me the Maltesers.'

Trowels at the ready. We're going in.

LEEKS

[ANNUAL]

| Seedlings | September–October | Full sun/part shade | 15cm apart | May–July |

For most of my life, I underestimated leeks. They never found their way onto my shopping list. Failed to ignite my imagination on a restaurant menu. Which reveals me for the fool I am. It turns out, leeks are one of the greatest vegetables on the planet – mainly thanks to my discovery of melty leeks and cheese on toasted sourdough (see page 143). Holy Cheddar, it's good.

I first planted a single leek on a whim. I was on a 'Buy One Get Four Free' rampage and decided I could squeeze in another plant. Whim, or the hand of the vegetable gods? Divine intervention, surely? I haven't looked back since.

TO PLANT

WHEN: You'll find leek seedlings in garden centres at the end of the summer.

WHERE: A sunny, well-drained spot in the garden.

HOW: Before planting, thoroughly dig over your soil with a fork, adding lots of compost and well-rotted manure. This will replenish nutrients lost to the summer vegetable crop, help with drainage and generally make your veg patch a happy horticultural place once more.

Planting leeks is surprisingly fun. First of all, make a 15cm-ish deep hole for each plant. Then drop your leek plant, roots down, into its little hole and fill the hole with water. I know! Grown-up mud-pie-making. Don't worry about closing the hole with soil – it all magically sorts itself out in its own time. And that's it. Leeks planted.

SPACE: Leave 15cm between each plant. If you're planting more than one row, leave 30cm between each so they have room to breathe.

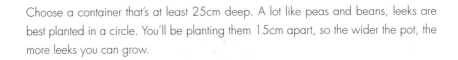 Choose a container that's at least 25cm deep. A lot like peas and beans, leeks are best planted in a circle. You'll be planting them 15cm apart, so the wider the pot, the more leeks you can grow.

Fill with good-quality potting compost to two-thirds of the height of the pot, then follow the planting instructions above.

KEEPING THEM ALIVE

Leeks have very shallow roots, so they become particularly angry if their soil dries out on a sunny day. The aim is to keep them regularly watered, but not waterlogged.

Apart from that, it's a good idea to add a little fertiliser into the mix. A couple of weeks after planting, sprinkle some tomato feed over their heads. A few weeks after that, scatter a few handfuls of bonemeal onto the soil around them. This should set them up for a long and productive winter's growing.

Then there's just one more thing. Blanching.

What is this 'blanching', I hear you cry? I cried the same thing the first time Timmy's granddad told me about it. Luckily, he's a kind and patient man in the face of horticultural idiocy. Topline: it's a clever trick for making your leeks grow longer white stem sections (the tastiest bit of the plant). To do this, simply 'draw up' the surrounding soil in a pile around the base of the stems, being careful not to get any between the leaves or it'll be a RIGHT palaver to get out in the kitchen. In pots, simply tip in more soil to raise the surface level as they grow.

HARVESTING

WHEN: Leeks don't mind hanging around in the ground until they're needed, which is very understanding of them. Start lifting a few while they're still young to ensure a long harvest period, from early spring, when they're at the 'large spring onion' size.

HOW: To lift, don't just yank them out of the bed. Using a fork, gently dig underneath your intended leek friend and gently lift him from the soil with a slow wiggly movement. You'll notice I used the word 'gently' twice there. It's no mistake. Leeks are delicate characters and if you accidentally snap the end off, how the hell are you going to Instagram your leek-shaped prowess to the world? A stark warning indeed.

HOW OFTEN: As needed, until they're gone. A sad day.

POTENTIAL DISASTERS

On the whole, as long as you don't let them **dry out** or become **waterlogged**, leeks are gloriously low maintenance. Which is good news, 'cos who wants to keep trudging out in the rain and snow all winter to look after them?

There are, however, a few **fungi and pests** that could affect them if you're particularly unlucky. **Leek rust** is the most likely, but mild attacks won't harm your leeks too badly. Unfortunately, there's no cure, so if you get a particularly bad attack put the plant in the bin and don't plant leeks in the same spot next year.

FROM THE GARDEN TO THE TABLE

MELTY LEEKS AND CHEESE ON SOURDOUGH

Serves 2

This is one of those recipes that somehow adds up to a hundred and fifty times more than the sum of its simple parts. I don't know quite what happens between the saucepan and the grill, but mark my words . . . tastebud alchemy occurs. Comforting, sweet, savoury and salty – 'tis a thing of wonder.

Here's what you'll need:

25g lightly salted butter

2 medium leeks, trimmed, washed and sliced

2 great big slices of sourdough

50g (or more…) really mature Cheddar, grated

Sea salt

Black pepper

In a heavy bottomed saucepan, melt the butter over a medium heat. As soon as it starts to foam, tip in all the leeks and wait for them to start sizzling. Turn the heat down low, pop a lid on, and leave to sweat gently for 10ish minutes until soft, tender and irresistible. Take the lid off and stir with a wooden spoon to make sure they don't stick at the last minute. When ready, turn the heat off, season to taste, then set to one side.

Heat the grill to high. Now for the assembly. Carefully spoon the leek mixture onto the slices of sourdough, portioning evenly so that there aren't arguments. Don't worry if it reaches ludicrous heights that start to challenge the laws of physics – this is a messy, melty, fally-over sort of a dish and all the better for it. Top with grated Cheddar and carefully slide under the grill.

Grill until golden, bubbling and magical, then eat immediately. A dollop of Branston pickle on the side and I'm a happy Hollie.

ONIONS, SHALLOTS & GARLIC

[ANNUAL]

| Sets (posh word for onion bulbs) | September–November | Full sun/ part shade | 15cm apart | June–August |

The vegetables I use the most in the whole wide world. What a ruddy treat to be able to grow them in my own garden. For some reason, the fact that I buy them so often, in such quantities, made me think that they'd be hard to grow. Goes to show what I know. These pungent little fellows are as easy as those cress hair eggshell men you used to make on the windowsill at school.

We'll be using onion, shallot and garlic 'sets' instead of seeds – essentially tiny papery onions – as it's easier and more reliable than seed. We're beginners, after all. Let's give ourselves a break.

But where to find overwintering onion sets? I couldn't find them anywhere, having been told they'd 'gone out of fashion.' How can growing winter veg be out of fashion?! In the end, I found a big box of assorted onions, shallots and garlic sets on the Internet.

I'd suggest ordering late July onwards, as they sometimes take a few weeks to arrive.

TO PLANT

WHEN: Now, strictly speaking, we should all be planting our sets in late September, but if you have a small garden it needs a little more juggling. My raised bed is full all summer long. If some of your veg (usually the tomatoes) haven't finished, don't panic. As long as you've planted your sets before the end of October, you should be fine.

WHERE: In a nice sunny/partially shaded spot.

HOW: Before doing anything, you need to replace the nutrients lost from the soil during the summer crop and turn it over to improve drainage. They don't like fresh manure (it can burn the young onion sets) so dig over the soil with a fork, then dig in plenty of high-quality compost and a bag of well-rotted manure.

After that, planting's easy. In a sunny spot, dig a shallow, straight trench for each row of onions, shallots or garlic. Pop your sets into the trench in a line, fat little bottoms down, pointy bit up. Then cover them over with soil, making sure the very tops of their pointy heads stick up above the soil line, in the fresh air. This always makes me laugh.

Handy hint: Remember to note down which varieties you've planted in which rows, and when each one will be ready (according to their bags). I keep a note on my iPhone.

SPACE: Plant 15cm apart and leave 25cm between rows.

A large pot is best, at least 25cm deep and as wide as possible – at least 60cm – so that you'll have space to plant enough to make it worthwhile. i plant my sets in a circle with one in the middle.

Pop your container in a sunny spot, then plant as above.

Handy hint: People have a lot of success growing these in tubs, which makes for an attractive container. You can find vintage metal ones in markets, or colourful plastic versions in interiors shops. Any tub really, as long as it's as big as possible - and remember to drill holes in the bottom for proper drainage.

KEEPING THEM ALIVE

Make sure you give your onions a regular watering in dry weather. Over-watering will anger them, but drying out will stunt their growth.

Other than that, regularly weeding between your growing crop is the most important thing you can do to keep them happy and productive. As your plants grow, you'll see how floppy and louche their long thin leaves are. Tall weeds easily outgrow and bully them, which will stunt your onion and garlic's growth, so every few weeks get in there with a hand rake and make sure all's clear between plants and rows.

HARVESTING

WHEN: It's easy to tell when it's time to pull up your crop. As soon as the leaves start to turn yellow and die back, they're ready.

HOW: You should be able to pull them out with your hands, by carefully holding on to the base of the leaves.

Before hanging and artful plaiting can commence, you need to dry out the onions and garlic a bit. In a warm dry place, lay them out for a few weeks (remember to keep their long leaves intact). Our little shed's sunny bar-sill is perfect, but a cupboard, larder, airing cupboard or under the bed in a spare room would be just as good. Check their necks every few days. If any are going soft, use these straight away. Neck rot is a terrible thing.

Once dry, move them to a dark, cool dry place . . . It's time to hang some onions. By far the most entertaining method is attempting to plait them, just as you would hair. It's strangely satisfying, and will stand all of us in good stead for future village craft competitions. But tying them up in a freestyle manner works just as well.

HOW OFTEN: Harvest the whole crop at once, once the leaves turn yellow and die. They'll happily keep for 3-6 months if you follow the instructions above.

POTENTIAL DISASTERS

Like leeks, onions, shallots and garlic are hardy sorts. Tom Hardy style. Hang on . . . I've had a moment. Tom Hardy. Where was I? Oh yes. Shallots and stuff. They don't fudge up too easily.

The main thing to look out for is flowering, or **'bolting'** to be scientific (if you've read the beetroot section, you'll be familiar with this term already). This is usually caused by cold temperatures in early spring, following their winter snooze. Pick off the flowers as soon as they appear and you should be ok, but here's an important and weird fact to bear in mind . . . though you'll still grow good onions (their necks will be a little thicker than normal) they don't store well at all. Eat them up straight away to prevent mouldy onion woe.

Onion downy mildew isn't as soft and snugly as it sounds. It appears on leaves as a white dusty powder, damaging the foliage but, most importantly, your precious tasty bulbs. They come out all small and weeny. There isn't much you can do, other than removing infected leaves, but there's all sorts you can try to prevent it. Sowing plants with enough space between each other, allowing lots of light to get in, weeding and making sure you don't over-water them should do the trick.

Leek rust is annoying but usually not too serious. It just makes your crop look a bit sorry for itself. After long rainy spells, you might notice a few bright yellow spots on the leaves. Remove infected leaves, and if possible, try not to plant onion, shallots, garlic – or indeed leeks – in the same spot next year.

Finally, **onion white rot**. I've left this to the end because, well, it's not good news. This is a dastardly fungus that causes yellow wilting foliage above the soil and rots the bulb and roots beneath. Disaster. And the biggest disaster of all? There's no cure. Dig 'em up and throw 'em out. Contaminated tools or boots are the most likely culprits for bringing in this rogue fungus to fresh soil. In an allotment or big veg patch, this is more likely. For us, with our pots and raised beds and small flowerbeds, it's less so. Fingers crossed onion white rot doesn't find you.

FROM THE GARDEN TO THE TABLE

MUMMY NEWTON'S DEEP-FILLED ONION TART

Serves 4–6 people

Here's what you'll need:

For the pastry

120g self-raising flour, plus extra for dusting

120g wholemeal flour

1 level tsp mustard powder

A pinch of salt

120g lightly salted butter, cut into cubes

80g extra-mature Cheddar cheese, grated

2–4 tbsp fridge-cold water (with more on standby if needed)

cont'd . . .

Yes. It's time for my mum to make an appearance. With an onion tart so tasty our entire family has developed a crack cocaine-like addiction to it. Rich onion, cheese in the pastry, mustard to give it a bite – perfect summer picnic fare. I believe it started life as a classic Delia Smith recipe, adapted by Mummy Newton to quell our insatiable onion appetite. This also marks our first foray into pastry. Rolling pins out, people. We're going in.

Pastry first. You can make the initial bit in a food processor – just whizz the dry ingredients with the butter. Or you can do it by hand in a big mixing bowl: sift both the flours (tip in the bran pieces), mustard and salt. Add the butter, then, using your fingertips, rub lightly until it looks like breadcrumbs.

Once you have your breadcrumb mixture (be it whizzed or hand-rubbed), stir in the cheese, slowly splosh in a little of the cold water at a time, cutting and mixing thoroughly with a pallet knife until the mixture begins to come together. Form the pastry into a ball with your hands then wrap in cling film and leave in the fridge for half an hour. Pastry done. On to the filling . . .

In a large heavy-based pan, melt the butter on a medium heat, then tip in your mountain of onion, stirring well to coat in butter. Add the sugar, then cook, lid off, for 30 minutes, stirring regularly, until the onions have reduced, softened and taken on a glorious caramelised golden-brown colour.

Preheat the oven to 180°C/350°F/gas 4 and put a baking sheet inside to warm up. Grease the tin. Meanwhile, on a clean work surface dusted with flour, knead the pastry and roll out to the thickness of a £1 coin.

For the filling

40g lightly
salted butter

900g white
onions, chopped

1 tsp golden
granulated sugar

2 large eggs,
beaten

110ml whole milk

A big handful
of chopped flat
leaf parsley

A scrunch of
sea salt

A good crack
of black pepper

2 big handfuls
grated extra-
mature Cheddar
cheese

A 20cm fluted
loose-bottomed
flan tin for a deep
tart, or a classic
25cm tart tin for
a wider, slightly
shallower version

Carefully lift the pastry into the tin, pressing it into the sides firmly. Leave any extra pastry standing up above the rim for now. Prick the base all over with a fork, line with baking paper or tin foil, then fill with baking beans or dry rice – something heavy to stop the pastry rising up. Slide onto your hot baking sheet and blind bake for 12–15 minutes.

Take your tart case out of the oven, then brush the pastry case with some of the beaten egg – enought to finely cover the inside surfaces. Return the pastry to the oven for 5 minutes.

Finally, the fun bit. Tip every last bit of onion into the now perfectly par-cooked pastry, spreading it evenly. Beat the milk and parsley into the eggs, season, and pour over the onions. Sprinkle the cheese over the top, neatly slice any extra pastry from the top of the dish, then cook for 25–30 minutes until the filling is fluffy, golden brown and irresistible. Enjoy.

SALAD

Is there anything more summery than a salad? Not the limp 1990s iceberg you'd find on the side of your scampi and chips, but the bright, fresh, bursting-with-flavour leaves you come across of a lunch at Ottolenghi's.

Chard leaves drenched in savoury–sweet dressing, wild rocket topped with freshly picked crabmeat, little gem lettuces charred in a pan. Fresh, crisp, colourful salad leaves available on demand from your garden.

Taste aside, the particularly glorious thing about salad is how easy it is to grow. I've picked a selection of the easiest for you to try in the following few pages. As ever, once you've got a hang of the basics, go wild. In fact . . . I've just ordered a packet of candyfloss pink endive seeds online. Outlandish.

TO PLANT

WHEN: In late April/early May you'll see seedlings start to arrive in garden centres, but on the whole, they're available throughout the spring and summer. Once you've harvested your first crop, you can go again.

WHERE: You'll need a sunny sheltered spot in your garden.

HOW: Little gems like healthy, nutrient-rich soil, so digging in a little compost or well-rotted manure before planting won't hurt. Give your seedlings a good water (especially at the base, near the roots) then carefully plant them in nice neat rows. Give them one last water for luck. A scattering of slug pellets is a very good idea.

SPACE: Plant 30cm from each other.

 If you're planting in a pot, you only need a shallow container (20cm or more), as lettuce doesn't have very deep roots. However, little gems get surprisingly big, considering their name. Try to keep seedlings 30cm apart to avoid arguments and ensure happier, healthier lettuces.

KEEPING THEM ALIVE

Keep them watered. That's my main advice. Moist soil makes for happy little gems. On a hot day I water them before work, then again when I get back in.

HARVESTING

WHEN: I like to harvest an entire head at once, when the lettuce is firm and suitably little gem-sized in the middle.

HOW: Use a sharp kitchen knife to cut away the lettuce at its base, a few centimetres above soil level, above the first few leaves. I often peel off the tougher outer leaves, but even so you'll find you have far more than you do from their shop-bought cellophane-wrapped cousins.

Leaving the stalk in the ground, with a few leaves still attached, often results in more leaves growing. I tend to pick these individually to encourage more growth. Bonus lettuce.

HOW OFTEN: Pick one lettuce at a time, when you want to eat them.

POTENTIAL DISASTERS

It's the damned **snails, slugs** and **caterpillars** you have to worry about with lettuce. Making sure the soil around them is weed-free helps, as it stops the little critters hiding during the day. If you suffer a **fly attack**, get out the Timmy insect spray (see page 30).

Netting will keep **Peter Rabbit and friends** from nibbling your lettuce, but we don't see him much in Shepherd's Bush, so mine have survived without.

RAINBOW CHARD

[ANNUAL]

Seedlings   March–July   Full sun/ part shade   30cm apart   May– September

How outrageously beautiful are these plants?! I'm still somewhat in shock that you can grow something so stylish and high-end-restaurant as this in your own garden or windowsill planter. Why does no one tell you these things?

While chard's leaves are somewhere in the spinach/beetroot leaf spectrum of flavour, their stems are far more similar in taste and texture to bok choi.

TO PLANT

WHEN: In bigger garden centres you'll find trays of multi-coloured rainbow chard from late April to mid-May onwards. As with little gems, you can plant a second later crop once you've harvested your first.

WHERE: Like the instructions for little gems (and, in fact, most lettuce varieties) find a sunny sheltered spot.

HOW: Dig in a little compost or well-rotted manure if your soil hasn't been replenished in a while and give your seedlings a good water before carefully planting them. Firm the soil around them, then give them one last water for luck. A scattering of slug pellets is a very good idea.

SPACE: Plant 30cm from each other.

    Chard doesn't need a very deep container but does like space to stretch his leaves. 1-2 per pot unless you have a very little pot.

KEEPING THEM ALIVE

Keep them watered. On a hot day, give them a quick water before work, then another before you go to bed.

HARVESTING

WHEN: At 8 to 10 weeks your chard's leaves will be big enough to pick and eat raw in salads. If you're cooking your chard, wait until the leaves have reached a bigger size, then cut to your heart's content. New leaves will grow to replace those you've cut. Like magic.

HOW: It's best to slice them off carefully with a small kitchen knife, a few centimetres from the base.

HOW OFTEN: Pick leaves as you need them for dinner.

POTENTIAL DISASTERS

Make sure the soil around them is weed-free, to eliminate **slug, snail and caterpillar** hiding places. Net the plants if you think you'll have free-range nibblers turning up in your garden, and keep an eye out for **aphids** and other **flying pests**. Timmy's bug-killing spray (see page 30) should sort them out.

WILD ROCKET

[ANNUAL/PERENNIAL]

| Seeds | March–
September | Full sun/
part shade | 10cm | June–
November |

Why rocket? Because it's super expensive to buy in the supermarket and only seem to come in a cellophane bag containing way too many to eat before they inevitably go over, rotting to an icky sludge in the bottom of the salad drawer. I've had it. From now on, I'm growing them. Especially now I've discovered how easy it is.

Why wild rocket? Well, seeing as we're growing it ourselves, I've opted for the punchiest, pepperiest option out there. However, the advice is the same for any rocket variety. Come with me, on a tiny rocket revolution.

PLANT IN A POT

 These are so successful when grown in a container that I wouldn't advise doing it any other way. Windowsill planters, hanging pots on balconies, big wide planters in the garden – all will work a treat.

WHEN: You can find packets of rocket seeds all year round. Sow from March to September.

WHERE: Wild rocket grows well in partial shade.

HOW: Fill your pot as normal – broken tiles/bricks/stones in the bottom for drainage, soil-based compost on top. Rake the surface to remove any lumps then sow your seeds, scattering them lightly across the compost. Cover lightly with soil, then water with a fine-headed watering can so they only get a sprinkling.

SPACE: About 3cm from each other.

KEEPING THEM ALIVE

Though rocket likes its soil kept moist, don't over water or it will dilute the flavour of the leaves. Weed between plants as they grow and, if necessary, thin out weaker plants to give their brothers and sisters more room to grow. In very hot weather, your rocket leaves need shade. Shuffle your rocket's container out of the sun to prevent the leaves becoming tough and unpalatable.

If your rocket starts to flower, gently pinch the flower head off between your thumb and forefinger. You want your plant to put all its energy into making leaves.

HARVESTING

WHEN: Wild rocket works best as a 'cut-and-come-again' crop.

HOW: Simply pick the leaves youwant straight from the soil with your fingers.

HOW OFTEN: From four weeks onwards, get in there and pick a few leaves from each plant. Regular picking will ensure a constant supply of fresh, young, tasty leaves throughout the spring and summer. Yum.

Handy hint: Repeat-sowing salad leaves will ensure a continual crop throughout the spring and summer. Sow every 1–3 weeks (check packet) and just as you've finished picking the first batch, the next leaves will be ready. I'd love to say that I'm a diligent repeat sower but I'm so forgetful that the ONLY way I've managed to do this is to set a reminder on my iPhone. Modern gardeners, eh?

POTENTIAL DISASTERS

Personally, the greatest problem I've ever had with my rocket is the **damned squirrel,** the arch villain of my garden. Only last week he dug up ALL my newly sprouted rocket seedlings. I've put a net over mine now. Thank goodness they grow so fast . . .

RADISHES

[ANNUAL]

| Seeds | April–July | Full sun/part shade | 2.5cm | May–August |

Radishes are so easy to sow that we're stepping into the world of seeds once more. Rip open that seed packet radish fans. From early spring through to late summer, these are the ultimate small-space container salad.

Handy hint: Radishes are so fast-growing that they're ready to pick a remarkable four weeks after sowing. The ultimate choice for an impatient gardener.

PLANT IN A POT

Radishes grow so quickly and reliably in pots that I tend to keep my raised bed for bigger, more demanding crops.

WHEN: You can find packets of radish seeds all year round. Sow from April to July.

WHERE: If you don't want to grow them in a pot, they thrive in beds too, particularly planted between crops that take longer to grow. Radishes will grow in partial shade but they thrive in full sun.

HOW: Fill your pot as normal, place some broken tiles/bricks/stones in the bottom for drainage and fill with a soil-based compost. Rake the surface to remove any lumps, sow your seeds roughly 5cm deep, then cover lightly with soil and water with a fine-headed watering can.

SPACE: Sow your seeds roughly 2.5cm apart.

KEEPING THEM ALIVE

Keeping the soil moist (not soggy, not dry) will ensure that they grow quickly, taste their best and don't split open. If you sow seeds in the middle of a heatwave, pay extra special care.

HARVESTING

WHEN: When your radishes reach roughly 2.5–3cm in diameter (their heads poke out of the surface so it's easy to tell).

HOW: Gently pull them from the soil. Ta da! Radishes harvested.

HOW OFTEN: As needed for dinner.

POTENTIAL DISASTERS

Not picking them soon enough will result in a '**woody' radish.** No one wants that. I pick mine when they're small and sweet.

If they seem to be getting a bit **close for comfort**, thin them out a little – 5cm between each radish should stop arguments.

If something starts to go awry, remove any **bugs** by hand/with our homemade bug spray (see page 30), and in a total emergency simply lift the offending radish and sow some more.

FRUIT

Luxury. That's the truth of it. Growing the ingredients for a thousand puddings under the guise of 'home-grown goodness'. Not that there's anything wrong with a homemade pudding from time to time. In fact, it's one of the main upsides to being a human.

It's difficult to be sad when eating a bowl of hot baked apple with caramel sauce and custard. It's also tricky not to have a ruddy good time when drinking fresh strawberry daiquiris in the garden with your closest chums, refusing to go indoors even after the sun has gone to bed.

The following are, in my experience, the easiest crops to grow for fast, fruity, reliable results straight off the bat. Happy eating, fruit fans.

STRAWBERRIES

[PERENNIAL]

| Seedlings | May–June | Full sun/ part shade | 30cm | July–August |

Aka 'pudding'. Strawberry season sees me longing for a proper strawberry bed in a massive great allotment – heady cravings driven by strawberry greed. Though they grow excellently in the ground, my garden is busting at the seams. So what to do?

Construct my own cunning strawberry containers, that's what.

I've tried all sorts of pots and planters, with varying degrees of success. But by far the most successful, and easy, method I've come across is . . . growing strawberries in a wooden wine box. Dead classy. I mean, most of them come from actual genuine France. Yes, France. Grab me a Pernod and call me Claude . . . these are some good-looking containers.

I found my wine boxes by trundling round the corner to the local off-licence, where they were piled up in front of the counter. Mine for the princely sum of £2 to their local charity. If you can't find any at your local offy, you can easily order them on the internet – though they'll be a bit more expensive.

HOW TO GROW

WHEN: Trays of little strawberry plants arrive in garden centres, DIY stores and even the odd corner shop between April and May. I generally buy 'strawberries'. There's rarely more information than that.

WHERE: A warm, sunny, sheltered spot.

HOW: If there's one thing strawberries don't like, it's being waterlogged. If you're growing yours in a wine box, the first thing to do is drill a load of holes in the bottom. Truth be told, I got Tim to drill them. I'm too clumsy to trust myself with power tools.

For bed planting, turn over the soil with a garden fork, dig in some well-rotted manure and pop the little fellas in. I tend to offset mine in two horizontal rows, to make the most of the space.

SPACE: Plant 30cm apart.

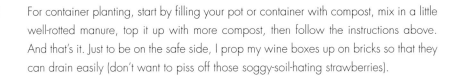

For container planting, start by filling your pot or container with compost, mix in a little well-rotted manure, top it up with more compost, then follow the instructions above. And that's it. Just to be on the safe side, I prop my wine boxes up on bricks so that they can drain easily (don't want to piss off those soggy-soil-hating strawberries).

KEEPING THEM ALIVE

Once your strawberries have started flowering (an exciting moment, I can tell you), they like a good sprinkle of tomato feed, mixed properly in a watering can, every ten days or so. This encourages bigger, fatter, juicier strawberries. Huzzah.

Strawberries growing in boxes, pots and hanging baskets like to have a quick water every day. Thanks to that brilliant drainage, they can quickly dry out in hot weather.

If you're growing your strawberries in the ground, you'll need to put a traditional layer of straw, or more modern sheet of polythene, underneath the plants to prevent the strawberries touching the ground and rotting as the fruits form. If you've opted for a wine box or container, simply hook your strawberries over the edge.

Then keep an eye on them and watch in awe as they start to turn red. Nature, eh? It's bloomin' magic.

HARVESTING

WHEN: As soon as they turn red all over. The one thing to watch out for is leaving ripe strawberries on the plant too long. They rot very quickly once ripe and can encourage disease, so get picking. This is easily solved by eating them. Every single day.

HOW: Strawberries couldn't be easier to pick. Hold them gently by the stem and pull. I almost feel silly writing it.

HOW OFTEN: Check every day and pick any ripe strawberries you can see.

POTENTIAL DISASTERS

Birds and **squirrels**; the terrorists of the garden. Like me, they love strawberries, and have been known to sneak them from the plant ten seconds after I turn my back. Luckily, they're scared of netting. Secure a piece of fruit netting loosely over your strawberry friends and the dastardly birds and squirrels won't come near them. Idiots.

Strawberry 'splitting' is the other woe that could befall your crop. Heavy rain followed by cooler weather seems to be the main cause. The best way to avoid this is drainage. Good holes in the bottom of your container, raised off the ground, or well turned over soil before planting in beds. (plus a prayer to the weather gods) is your best form of protection.

FROM THE GARDEN TO THE TABLE

FRESH STRAWBERRY DAQUIRIS

Serves 4

Careful. In my worryingly vast experience, one of these leads to another. And another. And another. Followed by bad behaviour, misjudged actions and strawberry remorse. This recipe uses strawberry liqueur to really boost the strawberryness. If you can't find any, the recipe works fine without. This is the stuff British summer time is built on.

Here's what you'll need:

16 fresh strawberries, plus 2 cut in half to garnish

8 tsp white sugar

140ml white rum

2 tbsp strawberry liqueur

100ml fresh lime juice (about 4 limes' worth)

A couple of handfuls of crushed ice

This couldn't be easier. In a large cold cocktail shaker (I often store one in the freezer in the hours leading up to a party) slice in your strawberries, mush them up with a fork/teaspoon, add all the other ingredients, mush it all up some more, add the crushed ice, then pop the lid on.

Shake it like a Polaroid picture.

Strain into two trendy Martini glasses, jam jars, tumblers – shoes, for all I care – and serve with an insouciant smile and strawberry halves perched on the rim.

RHUBARB

[ANNUAL]

| Plants | October–November | Full sun/part shade | 75cm | May–August |

Did you know that rhubarb is actually a vegetable? The world's gone mad! Just like my thoughts on tomatoes, I'm sticking to my guns here. A sweet vegetable? I'm keeping it here in Fruit, where I can keep an eye on it.

Not only is rhubarb lip-smackingly tasty, but it's very beautiful too. Tall pink stems and enormous, architectural bright green leaves that add an almost tropical touch to the garden. Which is lucky, because Mr Rhubarb is currently residing in my flowerbed. However, now that I've been forced to start growing produce in my 'ornamental' flowerbed, I've realised how attractive it looks.

There are lots of varieties of rhubarb plant to choose from – Champagne, Timperley, Stockbridge Arrow – and they're all delicious and available from most garden centres in late spring/early autumn. Simply pick the plant you like the look of most if you only have room for one.

N.B. Rhubarb plants are look-after-themselves easy to maintain, but mark my words . . . it's also absurdly easy to kill them – as I myself did – in the first year (see Harvesting). Luckily, you can learn from my rhubarb fool-ish mistake.

TO PLANT

WHEN: Rhubarb plants (known as 'crowns' in professional circles) like to be planted in the autumn, while the soil is warm and moist but hasn't yet frozen. I like to play it safe when I've just bought an expensive new plant, though, so ideally aim for October.

WHERE: Rhubarb prefers the sunshine, but it does surprisingly well in part shade – which is where I've had mine these past three years. They hate to be disturbed, so make sure the spot you choose is going to be Mr Rhubarb's 'forever home', then he'll produce a reliable crop for up to ten years if happy. Ideally, your soil will be moist and well drained.

HOW: Before planting, I like to help my soil along by digging it over thoroughly with a fork, mixing in plenty of well-rotted manure to a depth of about 60cm. Dig a hole a little bit wider than the plant, then drop in the rhubarb so it comes either up to, or around your plant. Gently firm the soil around the base and water well.

SPACE: With a leaf span of about 1m, make sure there's lots of space between each plant – at least 75cm so they don't start fighting. This is why I grow mine in the flowerbed.

Rhubarb needs space. It has a large root system and big old leaves, so any container needs to be able to hold at least 40 litres of compost to produce a proper crop (aka enough for a crumble). A reclaimed whiskey barrel would be perfect, but the rest of the world seems to have cottoned onto this too, hence their extortionate price. A metal vegetable oil barrel procured from your local Indian takeaway would work a treat. Or a plastic barrel, painted with brightly coloured exterior paint. There are even big 'rhubarb kit' grow bags on that there Internet.

Then follow the instructions as above. Use a soil-based compost mixed with plenty of well-rotted manure, and off you go.

KEEPING THEM ALIVE

Rhubarb's a happy little soul. Once up and running, he's super low maintenance – chilling out underground in winter after his foliage has died off, shooting up again in spring. To encourage a strong, steady supply of sweet, sweet stems, these two simple tips will make him even happier.

1. Pack in some well-rotted manure around the crown of the plant as winter approaches. Essentially you're tucking your rhubarb into bed until spring and replenishing the soil with nutrients.

2. When spring comes round, you might see some pretty little white flowers start to grow from your 'barb. Kill them immediately! Not out of malice, but to protect your precious rhubarb crop. Allowing flowers to set seed will weaken the plant by sapping energy, so snip off the flowers and seed stalks to protect your future rhubarb crumbles.

In the long term, to keep your rhubarb healthy, plants should be divided every five to six years during winter. Each plant can be split into three or four separate 'crowns' with a good old garden spade. Make sure each crown has a large bud or 'eye' – this will turn into next year's shoots. Like magic.

Then it's easy. Dig a hole slightly larger than your newly divided plants, then pop in the crown with his roots facing downwards. The top of the crown should be 2.5-ish cm below the surface, then cover. It's a good idea to mark where the new crown has been planted, with a stone or something equally cunning – then you can check that he's survived come February/March. With any luck, you should see new healthy shoots start to poke their heads out of the ground.

HARVESTING

WHEN: Stems should be at least 10cm long (though I aim for 30cm or taller).

HOW: Harvesting is simple. Simply hold tight at the base and pull/twist at a gentle angle in one move.

However . . . here's the highly important thing you need to know about rhubarb – **don't pick a single stem in the first year**. Even when they're right there in front of you, looking all pink and delicious. In the first 12 months,

This is how I killed my first, dearly departed rhubarb. I dont know if I'll get over the guilt. Mr Rhubarb is establishing himself. Don't piss him off. I risked it and took three strong stems in the second year, but I didn't dare in the first. I'd had the fear of god drummed into me by every rhubarb forum ever (I know how to spend my free time).

From year three, you can harvest rhubarb from May all the way through to August with abandon. For years and years. Lecture over.

Important note: never remove all of your rhubarb's stems at once, or he'll die a sudden and terrible death. In fact, I wouldn't advise removing more than half the plant in one go. Those leaves are the only power source for growing more fruit.

Second important note: don't be the jam fool who eats the rhubarb leaf. Stems yummy, leaves highly poisonous. Put them in the compost where they can't cause trouble.

HOW OFTEN: I pick one or two stems at a time, as they reach full size.

It's important to celebrate a big haul. Upon harvesting a particularly big stem of rhubarb, I suggest marking the occasion in traditional style by standing under it like an umbrella.

POTENTIAL DISASTERS

Easy-going rhubarb hardly suffers from any diseases. The incident you're most likely to encounter is **crown rot**, particularly if soil conditions are wet. Crown rot is a fungal infection that sneaks in at the base of the stalks, turning them brown and soft at the crown. Disaster.

Alas, there's only one thing for it. Dig up the whole plant and destroy it immediately (aka throw it in the bin). Fertile, well-drained, weed-free soil is the best protection. Stupid crown rot.

FROM THE GARDEN TO THE TABLE

RHUBARB COMPOTE

Having a perfect rhubarb compote recipe up your sleeve will see you through a lifetime of rhubarb seasons. On your yoghurt in the morning, with ice cream as a quick pudding, laced through cheesecake, even served with pork instead of apple sauce. This is so versatile, and so easy, you'll never stop making it once you start.

Here's what you'll need:

500g rhubarb (roughly 4 large, or 8 small stalks), trimmed and cut into 3cm chunks

160g caster sugar

½ thumb-sized piece of ginger, grated

1 tbsp lemon juice

2 tbsp water

Tip all of your ingredients into a heavy-bottomed saucepan along with 2 tablespoons of water and place over a low heat. Cover with a lid and wait for it to start simmering.

Once simmering, stir every now and then for 10–12 minutes, until the rhubarb is soft and tender. Remove from the heat and tip into a bowl, allowing to cool before you cover and pop in the fridge.

Stewed rhubarb will keep in the fridge for 5–7 days, or you can store it in the freezer, in separate freezer bag portions, for up to a year.

RHUBARB VODKA

Makes 1 litre

Here's what you'll need:

600g rhubarb stems

200g caster sugar

½ thumb-sized piece of fresh ginger, peeled and roughly cut into matchsticks

1 litre good-quality vodka

A sterilised (see page 100), airtight bottle – preferably 1.5–2 litres in capacity (a Kilner-type jar is ideal

Rhubarb's not just for eating. Oh no. It's for drinking, too. In the glorious form of ice-cold rhubarb vodka. Drunk neat. As a shot.

This recipe is short on prep, long on infusion – 6–8 weeks long, to be (sort of) precise. Wash your rhubarb thoroughly, lop off any untidy ends and chop into 1cm discs. Pop your newly sliced rhubarb into the jar.

Add the sugar, chopped ginger and vodka, then seal it tight, give it all a good shake, then store in a dark cupboard for at least 6–8 weeks. If you forget and stumble across it 11 weeks in, fear not, the longer it's left to steep, the deeper the flavours will be.

Over these rhubarb-infusing weeks, try to remember to turn or gently shake your brew every so often. Finally, at the end of all that waiting, strain the vodka through a square piece of muslin and transfer to a screw-top glass bottle. Rhubarb vodka will keep for up to 1 year.

Serve super-chilled in shot glasses on a summer's evening. And lose all sensation in your knees.

RASPBERRIES

[PERENNIAL]

| Canes | November–March | Full sun/part shade | 60cm | June–July |

Tim is obsessed with raspberries. Stumble across them on a country lane and there's no moving him for 30 minutes. He's like a Labrador. So when we finally got a garden of our own, a raspberry bush was Timmy's main request.

Hilariously, a young raspberry plant looks like a stick. With a few green leaves stuck on the end for luck. But you'll get fruit from the very first year, and more the next, until a few years in . . . a real life raspberry bush has grown.

I was a complete fool and originally only planted one lonely little twig, at the shady end of the raised bed. Three years in, though bigger, stronger and far more fruit bearing, he's tiny! Not to worry, I know lots more these days, so you can learn from my faux pas and create a luscious raspberry bush of your own. Luckily, raspberries do well in large containers, so everyone's happy.

N.B. We're planting summer-fruiting raspberries, rather than their autumn-fruiting cousins. Summer fruits in the garden are a wonderful thing.

TO PLANT

WHEN: Raspberry canes can be planted any time between November and March, as long as there isn't a frost due and the soil isn't waterlogged.

WHERE: Raspberries like fertile, well-drained soil. Though they prefer sun, they do pretty bloody well in the shade, so are perfect for the awkward shady areas of a small garden.

HOW: Once you've chosen a new home for your raspberry chums, take a sturdy garden fork and break up the soil in a manful Gabriel Oaks manner. Seeing as you're already breaking both soil and sweat, work in some compost or well-rotted manure too to feed the soil. Then it's time to plant your raspberry canes. Water thoroughly.

SPACE:

Each cane should be placed about 60cm apart, at a depth of about 8cm into the soil.

This is another 'the bigger the better' container scenario. At least 60cm in diameter and as deep as your knee. Normal 'dug from the garden' soil is all you need. As with ground planting, it's important not to use pure compost as it dries out too easily in a pot. Before filling, put some large pebbles or broken clay pot pieces in the bottom for drainage.

At equal distances, a few centimetres from the side, plant six raspberry canes around the edge of the container (no wonder my one was so unimpressive) and water them well.

After three years it's best to move your container raspberries into the ground.

KEEPING THEM ALIVE

Feed your raspberries well, and they'll feed you – by growing more of themselves. This is the sort of maths I can handle. And eat. When spring arrives, add a good layer of well-rotted manure (or balanced fertiliser from a packet) around the base of the canes, then top with compost to help keep your raspberries' roots moist in hot dry weather. It's a good idea to water them with tomato feed regularly as they fruit. Bigger, fatter, happier raspberries. Job done.

Apart from that, the main thing to keep an eye on is watering. Make sure the soil never gets too dry, or too waterlogged, and they'll be happy little berries. If you're growing raspberries in containers, keep a particularly close eye on them when the sun's out. Soil dries out quicker in pots.

Pruning. For raspberries, it's super simples. All you need is a good sharp pair of secateurs or a pruning knife and some gardening gloves to protect against thorns if you're feeling delicate. I'm slapdash and foolish so tend to just dive in and come out covered in puncture wounds. In late autumn, cut every cane that's grown fruit that year to about 25cm from the ground. I know. Horrifying. Have I gone mad . . .? Of course not. This will encourage lots of basal shoots, and ultimately, a thicker, more verdant, raspberry-heavy bush the next summer.

Finally, support. I occasionally tie branches into place against bamboo poles to keep them neat.

Handy hint: Your raspberry plant is likely to send out 'suckers' along its root system, meaning that random raspberry canes might pop up in a completely different spot in the bed. If this new little rascal is further than 22cm from the main plant, dig him up and pull him out, severing this section. It won't hurt your plant, but will ensure energy is being directed to the right places.

HARVESTING

WHEN: Raspberries are ready to pick when they look like raspberries. Red and soft to the touch.

HOW: Ripe raspberries come off the plant easily when gently pulled. And that's it. Raspberries picked.

Raspberries don't keep for long, so eat on the day of picking or freeze. Like rhubarb, you can build up a good harvest over the weeks, ready to use at your leisure.

HOW OFTEN: Check every few days for newly ripened fruits, and keep going until you've eaten them all. Raspberries rot on the branch if left too long, going all gross on the inside. What a waste.

POTENTIAL DISASTERS

The most likely woe to befall you and your raspberry crop is a **pigeon attack**. The bloody bastard pigeon. I caught him pecking at one of my precious raspberries only yesterday, getting it all over the fence. But worse still, I witnessed a **squirrel** pick one off the plant, look me right in the eyes and run off laughing. Seems I'm not the only raspberry fan around here. Luckily, the answer is simple. Netting. Thrown over your plants and secured at the bottom.

Another likely attacker is **raspberry beetle**. If you see dry patches on your berries, at the stalk end, this could be a sign, but the main sign . . .? A disgusting white maggot inside your raspberry! Bleurgh. I distinctly remember biting into one in the woods when I was little. Gross.

Unfortunately there's not much to do except pick off infected fruit and hope for the best. Some gardeners use a pyrethrum spray when the raspberries start to turn pink, then again two weeks later, to prevent these little beetles. I haven't been unlucky enough to suffer from them yet, so am playing it fast and loose. *fate tempted*

Raspberry **cane blight** and raspberry **spur blight** tend to pop up under the same conditions. Weak branches and plants under stress or overcrowding are most susceptible but follow the 'keeping them alive' advice above and you can prevent these. If, despite your best efforts, either occurs, cut out and dispose of any affected canes.

Raspberry cane blight is the most serious. A fungal disease that appears in summer, withering leaves of fruiting canes and turning their bases dark brown – even splitting the bark. Wood becomes very brittle, so fruiting canes snap very easily, taking your carefully grown raspberries with them. As well as cutting out affected areas, it's important to disinfect secateurs between cuts so as not to spread the fungus. To be on the safe side, cut affected canes back to below the soil level.

Raspberry spur blight is also a fungal disease, but a far less nasty one. If you discover strange purple patches on your canes, you've got spur blight. It won't kill your plant, but it will reduce your crop by weakening canes and killing buds. Cut out the affected areas and pray to the raspberry gods.

FROM THE GARDEN TO THE TABLE.

FROZEN RASPBERRIES WITH HOT WHITE CHOCOLATE SAUCE

Serves 4

If you find yourself with a bag full of frozen raspberries at the end of the season (this can also happen after an over-enthusiastic raspberry picking session on a weekend walk), this is a ludicrously easy pudding to make. We first came across it at Mark Hix's lovely restaurant in Lyme Regis. This is my approximation. No human can resist a second pour of hot white chocolate sauce once it hits the frozen raspberries and makes a mini swirling mist in the bowl, so make lots.

Here's what you'll need:

A big bag of raspberries (about 250g)

300ml double cream

300g good-quality white chocolate

Get a pan of water simmering on the hob and place a bowl on top of it, making sure it doesn't touch the water. Into the bowl pour your double cream and add the chocolate. Turn the heat down and leave everything to melt for 25–30 minutes, running back into the room to stir every so often.

Once smooth, silky and so good you've 'tested' way more than is healthy, it's time to plate up. Pop the frozen raspberries into 4 nice little bowls and pour the hot white chocolate sauce into a nice jug for the table. Serve immediately, letting guests pour their own sauce.

APPLE TREE

[PERENNIAL]

Young tree | September–February | Full sun/part shade | 75cm–5m | July–October

The great thing about apple trees is that they take years to grow, but start producing apples from a very young age. This means that you can take your apple tree, safely tucked up in his planter, from home to home, finally planting him in the ground when you reach your forever and ever house. They grow with you. Which is why they make an unexpectedly thoughtful wedding present. We've been giving them away left, right and centre for years.

You can buy ready-to-plant apple trees all year round from independent garden centres or have them delivered to your door from online suppliers. There are all sorts of varieties to choose from – Bramley, Braeburn, Cox, Worcester Pearmain – so the real question is, what do you want to eat? That's my sort of question.

N.B. You'll see both bare-root and container-planted trees for sale. We're going container planted as it's our first time. These are ready-to-plant straight into your garden; bare root plants arrive with no soil around the roots and have to be planted immediately. They are cheaper, but are only available during the winter months.

TO PLANT

If you're in your forever and ever house, these instructions are for you. If not (like me), skip to pots.

WHEN: You can plant apple trees at any time in the year, but they're happiest planted in winter.

WHERE: Find a sunny, sheltered position, away from 'frost pockets', and make sure it's in a well-drained area. Shallow or waterlogged soil is guaranteed to anger your little apple tree. Aka kill it.

HOW: Give your tree a good big water while it's still in its plastic pot and give the area it's about to move into a good water too. With a hefty garden spade, dig a hole a little bigger and deeper than the container your tree comes in, then pop him in.

Importantly, don't dig in any compost. Who saw that coming? Apparently it can soak up water from the surrounding soil and effectively 'drown' your new little tree's roots. Catastrophe! I'm not taking any chances. Backfill with the soil you dug out to fill your apple tree hole and all will be well. Job done.

SPACE: Depending on the size and cultivar of your tree, the space needed between two trees, or between it and any other nearby plants, will vary enormously. Refer to the label on your newly purchased tree.

Apple trees do very well in pots. The bigger the pot the better – at least 60cm wide, at least a knee deep – to allow your tree's roots lots of room to grow, before replanting him in a bigger container in a few years' time.

Apple trees don't like 'dug from the garden' soil in pots, so use a mix of compost and ordinary topsoil. As with planting in the ground, it's important not to use pure compost as it dries out too easily. Remember to put some large pebbles or broken clay pot pieces in the bottom of the pot to allow drainage before filling. Timmy's granddad recommends a decorative mulch on top – to keep things looking spick and span, hold down weeds and retain moisture.

KEEPING THEM ALIVE

Other than making sure your apple tree's soil is neither too wet nor too dry, the best way to keep your tree healthy is pruning. Yes, pruning. The glamour. The better pruned an apple tree is, the better the size and amount of fruit on the branches.

Horticulturally speaking, pruning prevents dead or broken branches from interfering with the new growth of fruit. Twigs or branches that are crowding one another or crossing over should be pruned. Use nice sharp shears, clippers or a pruning knife to make sure the cuts are made cleanly – at an angle so that water can run off the pruned area. Alongside dead, cracked, broken and dodgy-looking branches, twigs and branches growing in a downward direction should also be lopped off. Go ahead. Be brutal. Your tree will thank you for it.

As your apple tree grows up, training his branches will help to keep his shape looking lovely and make sure he's strong and healthy. As you train your tree you should be aiming, over the years, to give all branches freedom to grow without annoying and crowding its brothers and sisters. Keeping branches shorter at the top of the tree and longer at its bottom, will give it a classic look, allowing sunlight to reach every little bit. The simplest way to train the branches of a young tree is to tie them to each other, gently pulling the branches into place over time.

One final note: if frost is forecast and your apple tree is in a pot, wrap him up to protect him. A thick protective length of fleece or insulating material, wrapped around the pot will help, but popping him into a cool shed or garage on a bitter night will be even better. Though it might be cosy for you, never bring your apple tree into a heated house. That really will piss him off.

HARVESTING

WHEN: A ripe apple should have a firm surface and a crisp texture on the inside. If you're not sure, select a likely looking suspect and test him. That's science.

HOW: This couldn't really be easier if it tried. When your apples are ripe, gently pull them off the branch.

HOW OFTEN: Whenever you want to eat one. Pick regularly as over-ripe apples fall from the tree and rot, attracting wasps and wasting their appley goodness.

POTENTIAL DISASTERS

Apple trees are hardy. They manage to survive years of neglect in ancient orchards, then spring back to life at the hint of a cuddle. But the one thing guaranteed to fudge them up is too much (or too little) moisture.

If you see a **powdery mildew-type** substance forming on the leaves, it's likely that your apple has been exposed to too much dampness or humidity. Proper drainage is the answer. And a protected spot in the garden. Regular pruning should help prevent mildew too.

Apple scab is another, particularly gross-sounding risk. Perhaps unsurprisingly, this disease causes scabs to appear on the surface of your precious apples. Dark spots also appear on the tree's leaves. Once again, dampness is the culprit.

Then there are pests. If you start to see little tunnelled holes in your apples, chances are it's the work of a dastardly **larvae or maggot**. Eeeeew. Luckily, if this becomes a problem, there are traps specifically designed to stop them on that there Internet, imaginatively called 'apple maggot trap kits.' Go forth and order.

FROM THE GARDEN TO THE TABLE

A VERY BRITISH APPLE SAUCE

Makes a bowlful

Here's what you'll need:

200g apples, peeled and roughly chopped

juice of ½ fresh lemon

20g golden caster sugar

35ml water

A knob of lightly salted butter

A pinch of salt

Like good guacamole, once you make your own apple sauce and discover how quick and easy it is, you will never buy one again. It's illegal to have a roast pork dinner without a large dollop of apple sauce on the side, so this could well be the most important recipe in the book.

Slide the apples into a pan with the lemon juice, sugar and water. Heat gently until the apples are super soft, then squish with a spoon to remove any big lumps.

Add the butter and salt, mix thoroughly, then serve hot or cold. Your apple sauce will keep in the fridge, covered with cling film, for up to a week, or a year if frozen.

BAKED APPLES WITH HOT CARAMEL SAUCE

Serves 4

This takes me right back to winter evenings after school, when Mum would bake this pudding for my sister and me. Hot, fragrant baked apples, served piping hot with ice cream that melts the instant it touches them. A classic autumnal comfort pudding. I've added a hot caramel sauce on this occasion, partly because of my love for toffee apples, and partly because . . . well, you've grown these particular apples all by yourself. They deserve to be celebrated. N.B. I love sultanas, especially with cooked apples, but you can easily leave them out and stick with the brown sugar and nutmeg if you're a sultana denier.

Here's what you'll need:

4 apples that you've grown all by yourself, washed, scrubbed, peel left on

For the filling:

100g sultanas

50g dark brown/ muscovado sugar

25g lightly salted butter, softened and cut into cubes

1 tbsp Calvados/ apple brandy

A light grating of fresh nutmeg

For the caramel sauce:

125g caster sugar

250ml double cream

Ice cream, to serve

Preheat your oven to 180°C/350°F/gas 4. In a mixing bowl, stir together all the filling ingredients with a wooden spoon, or your (freshly washed) fingers. It doesn't have to be perfect, just approximately smushed together.

Next up, core your whole apples. My mum has a handy apple corer, but I make do with a small sharp knife. Pop out the core and then, with the same knife, score around the 'equator' of each apple, just breaking the skin. Stand the apples in a buttered ovenproof dish.

With a teaspoon and fingers, stuff the core-holes with filling, finishing with a walnut-size ball of the filling on the top. Bake for 30 minutes, until the skin is slightly golden and the flesh soft to the touch. If overflowing filling starts to 'catch' in the bottom of the dish while baking, add a splash of water. This will stop it burning and create extra sauce.

While the apples are baking, it's time to make the hot caramel sauce. In a heavy-based pan, heat the sugar over a high heat until it turns a deep, almost mahogany-gold-coloured caramel. Be brave; it isn't burnt. Stir carefully with a wooden spoon, making sure all the lumps are dissolved.

Take it off the heat and gently stir in the cream. Return the pan to a medium heat and stir to dissolve any last lumps of caramel.

Pour the caramel sauce into a nice jug so that people can serve themselves. Pop one apple per person into a bowl, with a massive great scoop of ice cream, and try to stop people fighting over the caramel.

FLOWERS

I feel I should admit something before we launch any further into this chapter. I was once a flower naysayer. A sneerer at blossoms. Laughing at the very idea of wasting precious outside space on something you couldn't, ultimately, eat.

Not for the first time, I was wrong.

Properly eat my words (and, as it turns out, flowers) wrong. A veg patch alone does not a garden make. From Michelin-esque edible flowers to rainbow-hued wild blossoms, there's a world of joy to be found in growing your very own blooms. And, it turns out, a particular stick-it-to-the-man smugness in abandoning the sad cellophane-wrapped bunches found in your local supermarket for something far more stylish grown in your own back yard. The sort of roses that would cost you a fortune in an upmarket florist; headily scented, nearly-impossible-to-buy sweet peas; hydrangeas that flower year after year, add structure to your garden and downright impress your friends when cut and put in a vase for a dinner party table.

Yes. My name's Hollie Newton and I am a flower convert. In fact – I may as well admit it seeing as we've come this far together – I've started to become dangerously interested in flower arranging now that I find myself inundated with the fuckers.

As with this entire book, I've drawn on my own experience when choosing which flowers to include. Impressive, stylish and abundant in their flowering, the following are, most importantly, very easy to grow.

1

EDIBLE FLOWERS

The delicate little blooms you find decorating highly fancy dishes in highly fancy restaurants – turns out, you can grow them yourself, right in your very own garden. Not only do they look beautiful but they are also fantastic in a posh salad. A miracle!

Pots, tubs, borders, the edges of containers already housing bigger plants – you can grow flowers all over the place throughout the spring and summer, using them to impress friends, family and Instagram in equal measure. Here's a handy list of easy-to-grow edible flowers for you to grow at home. Those with an 's' stand for flowers that need to be sown from seed.

Bean flowers (page 92)

Borage flowers (s)

Calendula daisies

Chive flowers (s) (page 60)

Courgette flowers (page 102)

Lavender (page 239)

Marigolds (calendula)

Nasturtiums (page 214)

Pansies

Pea flowers (page 110)

Roses (page 220)

Violas

Handy hint: We've already covered a few of the above, however, I'm going to give you some in-depth instructions for roses (page 220) and nasturtiums (page 214), because they take a little more effort and concentration. Borage, calendula, pansies and violas are easy-to-grow: last-one-season bursts of colour that I tend to grow in small containers. They'll all need good-quality potting compost, regular watering in hot weather and regular picking to encourage new growth. For seedlings, I plant one per pot. For seeds, follow the instructions on the packet, then thin out, leaving only the strongest, healthiest shoots.

MAKING THE MOST OF YOUR

EDIBLE FLOWERS

So what to do with your flowers once they start to bloom? Actually, it turns out they're hugely versatile.

Tiny little **borage flowers** frozen into ice cubes are a genius idea. My mum's, in fact. She's a cold drink renegade. Borage was, in fact, the original serving suggestion for Pimm's. A few leaves, a slice of lemon, and a couple of its beautiful blue flowers for colour. Try it. It makes for a refreshing alternative.

Sprinkling **chive flowers** onto summer salads in a louche manner suddenly makes everything look very River Café. Or you can use them for Chive blossom vinegar – pop whole flower heads into a Kilner jar of white wine vinegar, then wait until it turns a pale pink, giving it a shake every few days. The flowers give the vinegar a light onion flavour, perfect in dressings or on fancy fish and chips.

Little violas are excellent container plants, super easy to grow, last for months and months and don't mind being utterly neglected for weeks on end. All that, and they're edible too. Violas can be frozen into ice cubes, suspended into jelly, scattered over salads, crystallised in sugar . . . basically, anything that could benefit from a colourful flourish.

A particularly impressive way to showcase your edible flowers is on a cake, as demonstrated on this spectacular gateau by my friend Bee Berrie, of Bee's Bakery. If this doesn't impress your mother-in-law, nothing will.

The abve suggestions apply to all of the flowers listed on page 210, but there's one in particular that's so rampant, it's good to have some recipes up your sleeve for the inevitable hacking back you'll have to undertake . . .

NASTURTIUMS

[ANNUAL]

| Seeds | March–May | Full sun/
part shade | 30cm apart | June–
October |

Aka 'Edible Pest Control'. Black fly and caterpillars will attack the heck out of them, but they're so resilient that two days later, they'll be back to their tumbling selves. I plant one at each end of my raised bed to soften the edges and add a cascade of bright green and orange to my flagstoned garden.

WHEN: Sow nasturtium seeds in early spring and your plants will go all the way through the autumn and into winter, if it's mild.

WHERE: Though they prefer full sunshine, nasturtiums are perfectly happy in partial shade.

HOW: Rake the soil, then make 20mm-deep holes to sprinkle your seeds into. Cover with a light layer of soil. When seedlings appear, thin out if they're crowding each other.

SPACE: Thin plants to 30cm apart.

HARVEST: Once up and running, nasturtiums are so rampant that you'll need to cut them back quite brutally a few times over their growing season, to give space to your other plants. Luckily, the following recipes will mean it's a harvest, rather than a cull.

KEEPING THEM ALIVE: Nasturtiums are indestructible. In a drought, throw a bit of water at them, but other than that, they're a force to be reckoned with.

FROM THE GARDEN TO THE TABLE

NASTURTIUM FLOWER SCHNAPPS

Makes 750ml

Let's start with those deep orange flowers. Infusing their colour and peppery taste into a lean alcoholic base is a great idea and makes for a unique cocktail ingredient (or chilled after-dinner shots, Scandi-style). Its pale peach colour is irresistible and looks splendid sat on a shelf or drinks trolley

Here's what you'll need:

A big bowlful of nasturtium flowers

750ml schnapps (Doornkaat German Maize Schnapps, if you can find it)

A 750ml decanter, Kilner-style jar or glass container, sterilised (see page 100)

Choose the freshest, least-damaged flowers – shake off any bugs – but don't wash them. Then fill your sterilised decanter with the schnapps, drop in your flowers, giving them a gentle prod/stir around, seal and sit in a cool dark spot. It should take three-ish weeks for the peppery taste to infuse into the vodka.

Give it a try after a week or so. I like a strong peppery taste, but if you want a subtler effect, you might want to strain it sooner.

Then simply strain the liquid through a muslin-lined sieve, pour into a sterilised bottle and make some damn fine cocktails. It's particularly good served with soda over ice, a fresh nasturtium flower per glass as decoration.

NASTURTIUM LEAF PESTO

Makes about 150g

On to those big beautiful leaves. Nasturtium pesto is a thing of taste-bud-tangling wonder and a real treat to look forward to come nasturtium-cutting-back time.

I'll be honest, when I first came across a recipe I thought, 'what's this hippy shit?' But as usual, I was being an idiot. Nasturtium pesto is even more delicious than basil pesto. Stirred into spaghetti, sprinkled with Parmesan and accompanied by a chilled glass of white wine, this is summer in a peppery bowl.

Go forth and pesto.

Here's what you'll need:

1 big bowl (about 4 litres in capacity) nasturtium leaves

5 garlic cloves, cut in half

100g of really good Parmesan, grated

120g walnuts

A big big glug of extra virgin olive oil

A clean sterilised (see page 100) screw-top jar, about 150–200g

First, get in there and harvest the rampant little rotters. Don't worry about picking too many, it's like a triffid; more likely to kill you than vice versa. Wash all the leaves, then pat them dry on some kitchen paper.

Then it's easy. Chuck the garlic, Parmesan and nasturtium leaves into a blender with the walnuts. If you haven't got a blender, rip up the leaves and use a pestle and mortar. My stupid blender once broke halfway through, so I had to revert to cave man technology, and it worked a treat. Add the oil and mix thoroughly. When the mixture reaches a finely textured pesto appearance, it's done.

And that's it. Nasturtium pesto, ready in minutes.

Pop it in a sterilised (see page 100) sealable container and it'll keep in the fridge for up to 2 weeks. In fact, I'm going to eat some right now. Yum.

POOR MAN'S CAPERS (AKA PICKLED NASTURTIUM SEEDS)

Makes 200g

And finally, the seed pods from your nasturtium. Every single part of the plant going to good use. What a legend the nasturtium is. These taste so much like Italian capers that my mind went a bit boggly the first time I used them. In a putanesca sauce or caper berry butter, they're a direct substitute, if a little more peppery. Which simply saves on black pepper.

Poor man's capers are easy to make but do involve a two-day soak at the start. Just in case you were wanting to use them this evening . . .

Here's what you'll need:

200g fresh nasturtium seed pods

Cold water, enough to cover the seeds

1 heaped tbsp salt

200ml white pickling vinegar

1 tsp white sugar

1 bay leaf

A clean sterilised (see page 100) screw-top jam jar, about 200g

First things first, rinse the nasturtium seeds in cold water to get rid of any dirt or tiny insects. Tip the seeds into a small bowl and cover with cold water. Add the salt, stir well until it's all dissolved, then leave covered with a clean tea towel for 48 hours. This takes the edge off their peppery flavour, otherwise it's a bit overpowering.

When the two days are up, rinse the seeds thoroughly in cold water again, and transfer them into your sterilised glass jar.

Into a small saucepan, pour the vinegar and sugar and bring to a gentle boil, stirring gently until the sugar is dissolved. Being careful to get it into the jar, rather than on your fingers, pour the hot vinegar over the nasturtium seeds, right to the top of the jar. I find its best to use a sterilised funnel.

Add a single, artful bay leaf and allow to cool before screwing on the lid. Pickled nasturtium seeds will keep for up to 6 months in the fridge. What a brilliant find.

ROSES

[PERENNIAL]

| Plants | September–November, February–May | Full sun/part shade | 30cm–9m apart, depending on variety | June–October |

Truly, the Barbara Cartland of the flower world. I grow climbing roses over my fence and a beautiful David Austin 'St Swithun' rose that Tim gave me for Valentine's Day one year, in an outlandish moment of romanticism. Yes, roses are old-fashioned, but my goodness they're lovely.

Don't worry if your new rose seems to be nothing but a very expensive stick in a pot. Come spring, it'll burst into life. Promise.

TO PLANT

WHEN: Plant in early autumn, or in late winter/spring when all threat of frost has passed.

WHERE: Roses are happiest in full sun, but will grow happily in part shade.

HOW: Before planting, dig in a good helping of well-rotted manure and they'll be happy as clams. In early spring, dig a little slow-release fertiliser into the soil and a few big handfuls of bonemeal. Roses love bonemeal.

SPACE: Different varieties need varying amounts of space so refer to the label.

Follow the advice above and you'll have flourishing roses in no time – just make sure you don't plant them in compost. Ensure the circumference is at least three times the size of its original pot. Roses need support as they climb, so I constructed a sort of double arch for it to grow up, made from two tall bent-over metal frames. Cunning.

KEEPING THEM ALIVE

Water regularly. Sprinkle a bit of tomato feed on the roses, every two weeks. In spring dig in a good handful of bonemeal around the base. Deadhead weekly and trim back any over-excited branches.

HARVEST

Keep picking. The more roses you cut, the more will grow, so once yours are up and running you'll suddenly find yourself with so many on your hands that you become a WI version of yourself. Yes, it's time to talk flower arranging. I've been trying out some 'freestyle' vases recently – old wine bottles, mini milk bottles, espresso cups. Something modern to offset the old-fashioned beauty of those big flouncy roses.

2

FLOWERS FOR SHOW

I once got the telling off of my life for trying to feed a sweet pea pod to my sister, Alice. Talk about a misleading name; sweet peas are, in fact, highly poisonous. The edible flower section has ended, people. No more nibbling.

Instead, we're on to beautiful things for beautiful things' sake. Endless supplies of summer sweet peas, tall red tulips and cheeky daffodils to mark the start of spring, countryside musk mallow and corncockles. A garden fit for Monet.

SWEET PEAS

[ANNUAL]

| Seedlings | April–July | Full sun/
part shade | 30cm apart | May–August |

My favourite flowers in the whole wide world. There isn't a better scent in all of Liberty's perfume department. I like to keep a vase of them on my bedside table, as well as on the chest of drawers, and in the study, and the living room, and on my desk at work. There really is no stopping them once they get going. So let's get them going.

TO PLANT

WHEN: In late April/early May you'll see these seedlings arrive in garden centres, set out in big trays. Look at the labels, pick the colours you like best and bring them home quick. It's planting time.

WHERE: There's no getting round it, sweet peas need a bright sunny spot. They also love a rich, moist soil, so dig in some compost to enrich it and ensure that they stay moist during dry weather.

HOW: I swear, sweet peas grow taller by the hour once they get going, climbing up on their floppy spindly stems. Because of this, you'll need to construct some support for them. I've had my eye on one of those fancy wrought-iron cages for years now, but as it is I've resorted to those good old faithfuls, bamboo poles. Like peas and beans, you're aiming for a long thin Toblerone shape (see page 94), secured at the top, with a pole for each plant to grow up, at least 15cm apart in a row. When assembled, gently separate the plants, make a hole at the base of each pole and plant a seedling.

SPACE: Plant your seedlings 15cm apart from each other.

     The secret to happy sweet peas is allowing them a good deep, cool, root run. At least 45cm deep but, as ever, the bigger the better. Rich soil is perfect. Don't add compost, then simply follow as above. A tepee-shaped bamboo frame is what you need here.

KEEPING THEM ALIVE

As they grow, gently tie your sweet peas against their supports so they don't fall over. Keep them well watered (take it from me, I once went away for the weekend during a heatwave, arriving home on Sunday night to discover sweet pea genocide).

Handy hint: Sprinkle with tomato feed as they flower and your sweet peas will grow even more profusely.

HARVEST

Once they're in bloom, cut your sweet pea flowers every single day to encourage more flowers to grow. Snip any seed pods you spot. And remember . . . the more you cut sweet peas, the more they flower. Then you'll have flowers for weeks and weeks and weeks.

HYDRANGEAS

[PERENNIAL]

| Seedlings | March–May, September–November | Full sun/ part shade | 30cm–7m apart | May–October |

Hydrangeas. The blowsy, giant pom-poms of the garden. I can't help myself. I love 'em.

Found in garden centres across the country, spring and summer. I'm talking about the big classic blue, pink or elegant white variety. I started my first in a slightly bigger pot than the one he came in, perched in a Dresden milk churn I picked up in a market. Then, come the end of the season, when he started to look a little sorry for himself in his small pot, I planted him in the flower bed. He's been happy ever since.

One of the freaky wonderful joys of hydrangea owning is that the coloured varieties change colour depending on the soil pH. Pink in alkaline soils, mauve in a neutral soil and blue in acidic soil – so like me you might buy a pink hydrangea in a pot, and then watch it turn blue in your flowerbed.

WHEN: Plant in spring and autumn.

WHERE: In sunny/partially shady well-drained soil.

HOW: Dig some well-rotted manure or compost into your bed before planting, then water well – particularly for the first few days after planting.

SPACE: 30cm – 7m, depending on your hydrangea type and how much space you want to fill.

 Plant into a bigger pot than the one your hydrangea comes in, allowing it room to grow. Use potting compost and add slow release fertiliser pellets.

KEEPING THEM ALIVE

Hydrangeas, as their name suggests, like lots and lots of water. A water in the morning before work and later when you get in should keep them happy.

Though it's tempting to remove the brown paper-like heads of hydrangeas at the end of a season, try to resist the urge. These dead flower heads provide warmth and protection for their little friends growing underneath. In spring, cut them off just above the first pair of new buds on the stem.

HARVEST

Cut hydrangea blooms early in the morning, using secateurs to slice the stem at an angle. Plunge into water straight away to ensure that they don't wilt. Spectacular flowers, for free, from your very own garden.

WILD FLOWERS

[ANNUAL, BIENNIAL AND PERENNIAL]

Wild flowers don't have to remain in the wild, and you don't have to own a meadow to grow them. In fact, you can sow your own small-scale version at home with surprising ease. Scattering wild flower seeds is a particularly good way to fill gaps in your flower beds. Ditto large pots and planters. Being wild, they're good at scrapping to find light and exist quite happily alongside all sorts of bigger plants. Gawd bless'em.

There are all sorts of mixes and varieties of wildflower seed. Online suppliers sell everything from 'Wildflower Seeds To Attract Butterflies And Bees' full of intriguing names, such as **Yarrow, Lady's Bedstraw, Dark Mullion** and **Wild Red Clover**, to obscure Scottish heathland mixes.

In a local garden centre I came across a cottage garden mix, full to the brim with **cornflower seeds**, **musk mallow**, **ox-eye daisies**, **corn poppies** and **corncockles**. How very Thomas Hardy. This is part of the joy of wild flower seeds; you never quite know what's going to spring up come, well, spring. These days, I keep my eyes peeled and snaffle up packets whenever I spy one that takes my fancy.

WHEN: Your packet will give you precise instructions, but spring or autumn seem to be peak wild-flower-sowing times.

WHERE: Anywhere you like.

HOW: Simply rake over the soil lightly, water, sprinkle the seeds and cross your fingers.

SPACE: Refer to the packet for details, as each variety varies.

SURPRISE SPRING FLOWERS

[ANNUAL, BIENNIAL AND PERENNIAL]

I say surprise, because I'm so stoopid I always forget where and when I've planted my bulbs, and quite often forget that I've planted them at all. Come spring, I'm suddenly aghast at the **tulips, crocuses, bluebells, narcissus, alliums** and any number of beautiful bright flowers popping up all over the place. The solution is very easy. Write down what you planted, when and where.

Planting bulbs is both easy and peasy. Almost ludicrously so, considering the downright professional results the other end. But, as ever, there are a few hints and tips I've learnt along the way, to help you look like you've been doing this for years.

WHEN: Generally speaking, plant your bulbs in the autumn. Check the instructions on the back of the packet for precise preciseness.

WHERE: Pots, borders, hedges . . . even in lawns for smaller flowers such as crocuses, daffodils and snowdrops.

HOW: In beds, make sure the soil is weed-free and newly turned over with compost. If you have heavy soil, mix in a little agricultural grit to improve drainage. If you're opting for outlandish 'in the lawn' behaviour, remove the turf with a spade, place the bulbs underneat, roots facing down, and replace the turf. Don't cut the lawn until the plants have flowered and the leaves of the bulbs have turned yellowed and started to die back. They need those leaves to put energy back into the bulb for next season. Dig a hole 3–4 times as deep as the size of your bulb. That's it. Simples.

SPACE: Refer to the packet for details, as each variety varies.

 Pots need good drainage, too, so make sure you pop in some stones/brick pieces into the bottom, then add a good-quality potting soil.

Handy hint: For big dramatic flowers, such as alliums or large tulips, I have two tactics. 1: plant one in the middle of a pot, then plant lots of little flowers, like violas, all around the edge on top. 2: cram in as many as possible. A dozen tulips per 30cm container, as a rule.

VISITORS WELCOME

No, not random folk off the street, silly. I'm talking about nature, innit. Making a home that's just as welcoming to birds, bees and helpful insects as it is to us of a weekend. As luck would have it, a few small thoughtful actions can have a dramatic effect on our natural-world chums.

This section was originally part of the official Flowers chapter, so flower-filled is the bee-attracting advice. However, birds are just as important, and they're more interested in construction than growing. This means putting up birdhouses, as opposed to planting great big pompom allium flowers. *Lads lads lads.*

Right, let's start saving the world.

SAVE DE BEES

Now let's get this straight. If we lose the bees, we lose the plants. And if we lose the plants, we lose everything. At present, a third of the world's food production depends on bee pollination. Bees are, in fact, the world's most important and reliable pollinator of food crops — performing about 80 per cent of all pollination worldwide. And the bees are dying. You've most likely read or heard about the dramatic decline in bee numbers, but did you know that two species have become extinct in the UK since the beginning of the twenty-first century?

The causes are complex and inter-related. Pesticides. Drought. Air pollution. Climate change. Our bees' natural wildflower-rich grassland disappearing at an alarming rate. That's scary. Not just for the bees.

But all is not lost. Though you or I can do little to quickly effect political change into global agricultural policy, we can do our bit in our own back gardens, on our balconies and on our windowsills. There are 7.1 billion of us in this world of ours. If even a quarter of us started planting bee-attracting flowers like crazy, imagine the difference that would make. If all of us did . . . well, then we'd be getting somewhere.

Bees like flowers all year round: Spring, early summer, late summer, even autumn and winter if possible. When planting bulbs and plants, have a look at the packet or label. Is there a little 'bee-friendly' icon in the corner? Once you've found bee-friendly flowers, check when they're going to bloom. I've started to keep a stockpile in a box under my desk, in ascending order, all set to come out at different times of the year. Not only will this ensure colour in your garden all year round, but it will keep the bees happy for longer, too.

Climbing evergreen jasmine seems to be a particular favourite of the bees in my garden. They're like crack addicts around it. I love jasmine, because it grows quickly, needs little to no looking after and makes a garden look mature and verdant within only a few months. It also flowers right through from March to October. What a hard-working plant.

To plant jasmine:

[Perennial]

An evergreen variety will cover your wall or fence all year and look lovely even when it isn't flowering. Plant in full sun/partial shade in a sheltered spot, from early spring to midsummer. Before planting, dig in some compost, then slide the plant from its container. Water his root ball, then carefully pop him into a hole a little bigger than his bottom and water well. Pack him in with a little more soil. As your jasmine grows, loosely tie him to the fence or trellis that you're growing him against. Cut off dead flowers and branches in the growing season to encourage more blooms, feed with a little fertiliser every month and add mulch/compost in winter.

Bees like purple: Like The Artist Formerly Known As Prince, bees friggin' love purple. It's not an outlandish sartorial affectation, but real-life science; bees can see purple more clearly than any other colour. The first step in making your garden bee friendly? Grow lots of purple flowers.

To plant lavender:

[Perennial]

The more sun the better where lavender's concerned. It thrives in well-drained soil, so dig in a little sand or gravel if you're planting in a poor-draining bed. Plant young plants in April, 90cm apart. In a bed, lavender are very drought-resistant, so after the first few weeks you can water sparingly. As containers dry out more quickly, water pots regularly in hot weather. In September, after flowering, cut back the plant low to the ground, ready to spring back next year.

To plant alliums:

[Annual]

I grow mine in a tub – they're ideal as containers – in full sunshine. Small to medium-sized alliums can be planted closely together – 10-15cm deep and 10-15cm apart – to create a great big explosion of colour when they all come out. Plant bulbs in early autumn, ready for them to burst into life come spring/summer. Once the first growth has emerged from the soil, water two to three times a week, or whenever the soil is completely dry. Stop watering once the leaves die back. In a bed, alliums will grow year after year.

Handy hint: DON'T plant Buddleja. Bees (and their friends the butterflies) love Buddleja plants, but I'm actually going to advise against you growing any. This plant grows so quickly that it's difficult to control in a small garden. It is also the scourge of railways, and its seeds spread across towns, taking advantage all over the place. In fact, far from helping bees and butterflies, it can invade and ruin the delicate, varied wild habitats they love. Who knew buddleja was such a rogue? No buddleja for us.

Bees like trumpet-shaped flowers: In all their colourful glory, I've rarely seen trumpet-shaped flowers in bloom without an army of industrious bees shuffling their bottoms up the end of their bells. Tee hee. Why trumpet-shaped flowers in particular? They provide bees with a safe place to crawl up into and easily reach nectar. Foxgloves and honeysuckle are brilliant, hardly-any-effort choices for the beginner gardener, and the bees will be your best friends forever. Win win.

To plant foxgloves:
[Biennial]

Foxgloves can allegedly grow up to 1.8m tall, though mine have rarely made it past the 1.2m mark. They do very well in partial shade, so are ideal for an awkward shady spot. However, brace yourself for a little disappointment . . . foxglove plants don't flower until their second year. Foxglove plants can be planted in late September/early autumn and prefer a well-drained soil. Deadhead after flowering. Foxglove plants will last two years, but are very likely to self-seed new plants. IMPORTANT FOXGLOVE NOTE: foxgloves are poisonous to dogs, cats and even humans.If you've got errant pets, or indeed errant young children, make sure you plant them out of reach, towards the back of a bed.

To plant honeysuckle:
[Perennial]

Planted at the base of a wall or fence, climbing honeysuckle (rather than its shrubby cousin, because I'm guessing that you have a wall) will do just that – ramble on up and over, reaching for the sunlight, all the while covering a boring surface with bright green leaves and radiant, sweet-smelling flowers as it goes. Plant young honeysuckle plants in spring, in full sun/partial shade, with plenty of compost dug into the soil, and support with twine as they climb. Trellis or wire stretched horizontally in rows across the surface it's growing on will work a treat. Cut back any straggly growth after flowering in summer and they'll be ready to go next year, if topped up with a little fertiliser in spring.

Bees like fruit and vegetables: It's true. Not only do you get to feed yourself, you make the bees happy too. In fact, growing a thriving, diverse crop of fruit and veg is just about the most helpful thing you can do for our chums the bees. Tomatoes, broad beans, runner beans, sugarsnap peas, mangetout, courgettes, onions, shallots, garlic – all of these produce sweet nectar-rich flowers, attracting bees to your garden from miles around. The fruit we're growing is brilliant for bees, too. Apple blossom is one of the loveliest things about spring – I grew up with an enormous old tree right outside my bedroom window – and the bees go mental for it.

And a bee hotel: Did you know that lots of bees don't live in hives? Many bee species prefer to go solo, seeking out tiny spaces such as hollow stems and holes in deadwood – even in the ground – to make nests in. In a built-up urban environment these are hard to come by, so a bee hotel is a thoughtful addition to a garden, hung up high on a wall or fence that gets lots of sun in the morning. Filled with hollow tubes of various sizes, they provide a perfect hideaway for passing bees. They also look great, adding a bit of visual interest to even the most boring of walls, so it's good news all round.

SAVE DE BIRDS

Like bees, birds need all the help they can get from us humans at the moment. Yes. Even the dastardly wanker pigeon nemesis of mine. Though I'm mainly in it for Mr Robin. He's a dude.

Birds' natural habitats are being destroyed and encroached upon by the day. If I were a bird, I'd be thoroughly pissed off by now. Urbanisation has made it harder and harder for them to find food and a downright struggle to find nesting places. They're in trouble and, frankly, a world without birdsong would be a very sad and quiet place indeed.

But all is not lost. Dry your eyes. Wipe away that snot with your sleeve. Re-stiffen that lip. The good news is we can significantly change the fortunes of native and visiting birds in our own gardens, on our balconies and outside our windows.

Birds like food in winter: They like food in summer, too, but it's winter when our feathered friends really need our help, as there aren't so many insects around for them to munch on. The easiest way to attract birds into your garden is to put up a hanging bird feeder. Either a fancy one on a stick if you have real-life grass (the dream), or a wall-mounted feeder. The key is to get it up high, away from predators. Positioning your feeder away from your raised bed/veg patch is a good idea, too, to ensure that errant seeds don't fall in and start sprouting. Remember to wash out and clean your bird feeder every now and then. You don't want to accidentally spread infection. The guilt.

Different birds like different seeds, so experiment with a few mixes and see who turns up. Standard birdseed mixes, and slightly fancier sunflower seed mixes, have worked a treat for us over the years – robins, blue tits, great tits, sparrows, chaffinches and even wrens have popped by for a visit. The silly old pigeon waddles along and eats all the spilled seeds on the floor, but at least it keeps the mice away. We've splashed out on black nyjer seeds a few times, and lo and behold, greenfinches turned up for dinner. This is BIG news in bird-watching circles. Shit. I've become a twitcher.

Birds like water: Not only do birds need water to drink, they need it to splash about and bathe in too. Like over-excited toddlers. However, whereas many of us regularly put food out for birds, far fewer provide clean fresh water. There are all sorts of birdbaths available, in all different shapes and sizes. I don't feel old enough to have a stone birdbath in my garden – I'm not 90 – so I've rebelled and installed a vintage teacup and saucer, secured to a metal stick and planted in the flowerbed. You can buy hanging ones, old-fashioned stone bird baths (I'm not banning you), or simply put out a plastic tub of water. The birds don't mind what it looks like. The main thing to keep an eye on is the condition of the water. Regularly clean your container and replenish it with fresh water. When the temperature drops below freezing, warm water from the tap will stay un-frozen for longer.

Birds like a place to sleep: That Bitchin' Birdhouse (see page 47) isn't just for show. A birdhouse or two, positioned in the right place, can provide a proper home for a young bird family – protected from predators and the cold. As excitement goes, there's not a lot to top the discovery of REAL-LIFE BABY BIRDS living in a birdbox you put up especially. I can still remember watching the kamikaze baby blue tits learning to fly outside my bedroom window, from their home high up in the apple tree. I also have an open-fronted robin house, mounted super high up in the ivy at the back of my garden.

Different birds need different-shaped and -sized homes, so it's best to do a little investigating. Birds also nest at different heights. Placing birdhouses high up, away from predators and in a quiet undisturbed spot is best. Away from the feeder (they don't like to be disturbed by other birds). Then follow the instructions on the label. If you're lucky enough to have a nesting family in your birdhouse, make sure you remove the old nest after they've left, cleaning it thoroughly so that it's ready for the next family.

AND FINALLY . . . THE JOY

OF COMPOSTING

Yes. The joy, I tell you. Just look at my new compost bin – yes, it's pink and disguised as a beehive. Stop judging me. It's fabulous.

And useful.

I've put this at the end of the book because, for me, the desire to compost crept up on me over the years. As I began to hit my stride and plant more, I naturally began to generate more plant waste as different crops and flowers went over. After a few years of throwing away cleared dead plants from the garden, not to mention out-of-date food in the fridge, I'd finally had enough. Hence the purchase of the trendiest compost bin in town.

So why all the excitement?

One: you get to feel outrageously smug. Recycling food and plant waste as compost saves a bum-tonne of global-warming-inducing gases – it all goes into the garden instead of landfill.

Two: you get to make nutrient-rich food for your garden for free. Nitrogen, phosphorus, potassium; it's all in there. Feeding your plants, helping to improve soil structure, maintain moisture levels and keep soil pH in check. Hooray for compost! Not bad for a glorified dustbin.

But how to make the perfect compost? Are there rules? Are there terrible composting faux pas one can make? Of course there are.

As is often the way with gardening, it turns out that all sorts of people have all sorts of rules. Some of them quite vehement. So I've started, as ever, at the basic end of the scale.

As a guiding principle, aim for a balanced mixture of green stuff (plants, veg, fruit, grass, etc. – they don't actually have to be the colour green), brown stuff (autumn leaves, dead plants, straw) and other stuff (including hair, egg shells, even torn-up paper and clothing), but only a little of this. There are a few things that you shouldn't compost (diseased plants, citrus fruits, walnuts, weeds, heavily coated or glossy paper, and bread, milk, meat and rice based food) but mostly, just get stuck in there.

I recently composted all my summer veg plants – the courgettes, the beans, but not the tomatoes as their seeds are likely to survive and spring up all over the place. I've also added fallen brown leaves, all sorts of fruit and veg scraps from the kitchen, eggshells, hair (from my hairbrush. Weird.) and periodically stirred it around a bit. You need to check that it's damp (add a jug of water if it seems dry) and warm (use your hand – if it doesn't feel warm to the touch, add nitrogen/green stuff).

Now there's only one thing more to add . . . Wee. Apparently, there's nothing quite like it for kick-starting a compost. Which is why, tonight, Timmy will be creeping out to the garden under cover of darkness . . .

What a glorious way to end the book.

THE END

I know. It's emotional. We started out barely being able to hold a trowel and now look at us: nipping into the garden to water the beans before work. Amazing friends and family with our fried courgette flowers. Sitting happily in mismatched deckchairs, recovering from our hangovers while watching the bees get high on honeysuckle.

I think, perhaps, we might even call ourselves gardeners.

However, more importantly than this newly found gardening prowess, I sincerely hope that, no matter on how small a scale, we might all be just that little bit happier because of it. A little more calm. A little more connected to the natural world. Considerably more covered in mud. That would make me very proud indeed.

This book should keep you going for the first few years of windowsill, balcony, front step and garden adventures. Dip in and out. Use the chapters that appeal most. Try, fail, laugh, then try something else.

With any luck, I'll have written the next book by the time you get bored.

Until then, I'd love to see how you get on. Failures and triumphs. Teacher's pet peas and hilariously wonky carrots. (Again, not a euphemism. Social media has rules, people.)

Share your endeavours on Instagram, #HowToGrowBook @HollieNuisance

I'm off to the pub shed now.

Thank you for reading.

xx

INDEX